THE LEGEND OF
PAN PHILLIPS

THE LEGEND OF
PAN PHILLIPS

Jack and Darlene Brown

Floyd Eugene
(Pan) Phillips
at age five.

Canadian Cataloguing in Publication Data

Brown, Jack.
    The Legend of Pan Phillips

    Includes bibliographical references.
    ISBN 0-9617572-1-3

    1. Phillips, Pan. 2. Ranchers—British Columbia—Chilcotin River Region—Biography. 3. Ranch life—British Columbia—Chilcotin River Region. 4. Chilcotin River Region (B.C.)—Biography. I. Brown, Darlene. II. Title FC3845.C445Z49 1998   971.1'7504'092 C98-910214-9 F1089.C42B76 1998

First printing March 1986
Second printing January 1987
Third printing July 1988
Fourth printing November 1991
Fifth printing February 1998
Sixth printing May 1999
Seventh printing October 2000

Published by:

The TIMES JOURNAL PUBLISHING CO.
Darlene E. Melville
P.O. Box 1286
Puyallup, Washington 98371
Tel: 253-848-2779 Fax: 253-770-7369

Distributed In Canada by
Sandhill Book Marketing Ltd.
#99 - 1270 Ellis Street.
Kelowna, BC, Canada V1Y 1Z4
Email: sandhill@direct.ca Fax: 250-763-4051

Photographs courtesy of the Phillips family.
Cover design by Jim Brennan

Printed and bound by Kromar Printing Ltd.
725 Portage Avenue
Winnipeg, Manitoba, Canada R3G 0M8

FOREWORD

Re-structuring seventy three years in the life of a man such as Floyd Eugene (Pan) Phillips is a monumental task in itself, and in this case even more so.

For each segment of his life we have uncovered different versions, further complicated by rumour upon rumour. Tales of Pan's daring - do abound, embelished unsparingly from narrator to narrator. Sorting the wheat from the chaff, fact from fiction, was a major problem.

With the untiring help of many of those listed on the page of acknowledgements we have at last arrived at what we feel is the true story (biography) of Pan Phillips.

Regardless of what you may have read, or heard, we hope you will enjoy what we believe to be the factual version of his life and perhaps feel just a bit closer to this pioneer cattleman, guide-outfitter and resort owner, who's life became legend.

ACKNOWLEDGEMENTS

There were many people who contributed bits and pieces to the puzzle of Pan Phillip's life and we thank them sincerely; however, we feel we would be remiss if we did not offer special thanks to the following people, who made a major contribution to this biography.

listed in alphebetical order, they are:

Gus Abel
Ed Adams
George Aitkens
Peter Alexis
Rex Bartlett
Carol Berg
Dieter Berg
George Betemps
Veera Bonner
Alfred Bryant
Wes Carter
Toby Cave
D'arcy Christensen
Dave Dorsey
Frank Dorsey
Pat Dorsey
Steve Dorsey
Alyce Engebretson
Fred Engebretson
Harold Engebretson
Alex Fraser
Gertrude Fraser
Ila Graham
Gordon Hames
Linda Harrington
Kathy Hobson
Gloria Hobson
Dr. Alex Holley
Judy Holley
Donna Holley

Tom Holte
Caroline Howard
Margaret Johanson
Connie King
Art Lavington
Dude Lavington
Alf Legler
Bill Lehman
Dale Lehman
Mike Lehman
Leo Lillienwise
Ann McKilvington
Bill McKilvington
Jake Malic
Jack Maxwell
Donnna Mikkleson
Lizzie Paley
Gordon Pennoyer
Len Pickering
Wayne Reavis
Adelia Rybecki
Frank Sill
Alvin Simrose
Larry Smith
Bill Solowoniuk
Thomas Squinas
Jimmy Stohl
Alan "Shag" Thompson
Jack "Happy" Thompson
Bunch Trudeau

Sandy Unger
Floyd Vaughan
Rebecca White
Bob Williams
Gertie Williams
Gordon Wilson

And the Phillips family:

Ada Irene Cadwell
Al Biggan
Andrea Phillips
Barry Rempel
Betty Phillips
Diana Rempel
Elaine Biggan
Eva Willard
Gayle Simpson
Hazel Seeds
Helen Stephenson
Homer Phillips
Joe Phillips
Ken Phillips
Kim Magee
Melvin Phillips
Rob Phillips

> "Pan knew everything about his beautiful British
> Columbia, nature, animals and survival. Mix that with
> a great sense of humour and you have one of a kind, the
> mold is no more."
>
> ——Hazel Phillips Seeds

A COWBOY FROM THE WORD 'GO'

A son, destined to become, perhaps, the most famous cattleman on the North American continent, was born to Loren and Sarah Murphy Phillips, March 13th, 1910, at home in the family farmhouse, in Detroit Township of Pike County Illinois. He was christened Floyd Eugene Phillips, a name few would recognize in his later life. As he grew up, his middle name, Eugene, represented a 'moniker' that was too sissified to suit him,so he never used it except in legal matters such as when he became a Canadian citizen further down the trail.

Floyd Phillips was the oldest son, with three brothers and seven sisters. He received his early education in a one room school, called Goldman, walking a mile and a half each way to attend classes. Our research has failed to uncover a clue to his learning ability,or to his attitude towards being educated, but apparently he was above the norm, as he went on to attend high school in Pittsfield,Illinois, until he had finished grade eleven, a thing very few farm boys achieved at that time.

Details of his childhood days can best be told by his sister and brother in their own words.

Helen Phillips Stephenson, his oldest sister, relates, "Floyd liked horses at an early age. By the time he was fourteen, he had everything broke to ride, even the milk cows."

"We rode the old ram, too. He didn't buck, but he sure could make a square turn and we went straight ahead. Our entertainment in the winter was sledding and skating, in the summer, it was the old swim-hole."

"Floyd rode all the colts and mules before they were a year old,"Joe Phillips, his brother told us. "One time he got bucked off and broke his collar bone. He was at home alone at the time, and no one knew anything was the matter with him until Mother heard him crying in the middle of the night. When she got up to see what was wrong, he said

FOUR OF PAN'S SEVEN SISTERS are shown with him in this photo taken in the summer of 1919, when he was nine years old. (L,to R.) Helen, age 7; Mary, age 6 mo: Pan; Eva, age 2½years; and Vivian age, 4½years.

his shoulder was hurting, and then told Mom and Dad that he had gotten bucked off the mule."

From his sister,Eva Phillips Willard, "Although I was only nine years old when my brother, Floyd, left home, I have quite a few memories of him as we were growing up. He was a lover of the out-of-doors and enjoyed skating and hunting. He liked working with horses and had ridden all of our young horses by the time they were a year old."

"Many a Sunday afternoon, he would entertain a group of his friends by putting on a 'wild west show' for them. He spurred the horses until they bucked, sometimes throwing him off, but he usually rode them well."

"He was also good with the lariat rope and would lasso my sisters and me as we walked along. Before we were aware of his whereabouts, he would have us on the ground with one ankle surrounded by a rope. He spent many an hour practicing."

"In the spring of 1926, he was making preparations

with a friend, Johnny George of Griggsville, (who had a car), to go to Kansas to work during the wheat harvest. I remember, very distinctly, the day he left; it was June 1st. Mother was washing clothes on the back porch and Dad was also at the house, when he came and told them he was leaving. Mother shed many tears, but Dad was quiet and subdued as Floyd said his good-byes."

"The two boys, Floyd was 16, Johnny a little older, left and worked in Kansas the complete season, saving as much money as possible. At this time the two boys parted their ways; Floyd going on to Wyoming and Johnny returning to Griggsville."

After a long, hard summer's work in Kansas wheat fields; with his blisters turned into callouses; formerly, empty pockets jingling change; and some folding money tucked away; Pan set his sights further west. Since, Johnny had returned to Illinois, Floyd soon found new friends to travel with him, Floyd White and Roy Davis. They arrived in Wyoming, with still a few dollars, but no visible worldly assets. Riding the rods was the mode of travel in that era, and though no one remembers exactly how they got to Wyoming, everyone took it for granted that they came on the "Hobo Express."

While Davis and White landed jobs on the neighbouring ranch, near Crowfoot, Wyoming, Floyd got a job on George Pennoyer's Half Box E Ranch. Bob Williams' father, Mort, was the Half Box E foreman at that time, and Bob remembers his Dad being quite suprised at how the farm boy, from Illinois, caught on so quickly to the manful art of cowboying.

Somewhere in this time span, while still in his teen years, Floyd became known as "Wildhorse Phillips." a nickname that we are reasonably sure came about because of his eagerness and ability to fork any unbroken horse and give it quick education on carrying a saddle and a man on it's back, without instant rodeo action. Later, he picked up the alias "Panhandle Phillips", and much speculation arises over the possible source of this name. Here, we will go along with the majority, who feel that he earned the title, as an always broke, penniless, young man with an insatiable nicotine habit, which forced him to invariably 'panhandle' the makings of a cigarette, from strangers and acquaintances alike, and not from working in the panhandle territory of Texas or Nebraska. Hence, the nickname 'Pan' stemmed from 'Panhandle.'

To continue with family reminiscing, Pan's sister Ada Irene Phillips Cadwell had this to say, "I was born in April, 1925, and my brother, Pan, left to work in the wheat fields in June, 1926, so really I didn't get to know my brother until he came back home in 1929."

"Pan teased way back then. He told me my name was, Ada Irene, what makes you scream? He said this so often, I believed him. One day, when we went to Floyd Giger's home to pick up Dad, after he had finished cutting wheat with his horse drawn binder, Mr. Giger asked me my name. I told him 'Ada Irene, what makes you scream Phillips.' Mr Giger asked me several times and I repeated the same thing. Everyone laughed each time and this is why I remember it."

"My first memory of my brother," said his sister Betty Phillips Bradshaw, "was during his second visit home. I was about 10 years old. During this visit, we went to a photographer and had a family group picture taken. Our Dad died a couple of years later, so that was the first time all eleven children and parents were together."

" The return visits of Pan were also enjoyable. He, thoughtfully, made a point to do something nice for each of us while he was here. It ranged from giving us a souvenir to taking us to a restaurant. We always sat up late, usually around the kitchen table, in whichever home he was visiting, swapping stories and drinking coffee or tea."

Hazel Phillips Seeds, Pan's youngest sister, recalled fondly, "I first became aware of my older brother, Pan, through his short, but precious letters to our Mother. She looked forward to seeing his sprawling handwriting on an envelope. The letters did not come often, but he did keep in contact and sent her many pictures through the years."

"Our Mother was a very strong religious person and had a lasting influence on all of us. However, she was extremely superstitious and may have been responsible for some of Pan's superstitions, rather than an actual experience or incident. To this day, I will not leave on a trip on Friday and I never sew on Sunday."

Pan continued wandering in Wyoming. After he left Half Box E Ranch, his travels were not fully recorded, but the names of the Smith Ranch, the King Ranch, the Federal Ranch, Kirkland's JK Ranch, and the Diamond G Ranch, all have been mentioned as places he worked. Pan was fast becoming a top hand.

He did once admit to a friend, however, in later years, that he had spent a "bit of time" herding sheep in Wyoming, too, and stated,"After spending a summer in the mountains with sheep, you get spoiled because the dogs do all the work."

One story, though, did come out of the sheep herding episode.While tending his flock, Pan got lost in a summer squall and ended up in a mountain valley that he had never seen before. He spotted a log cabin, near a small creek, and rode over to investigate. No one was around, nor was there any sign they had been for quite a spell, yet the dishes were setting on the table, guns were in the racks, wood was cut and placed near the stove, and a bedroll was laid out on the tick, just as if the inhabitant had walked off moments before. Everything was old and dusty. Pan was spooked, understandably. He felt uneasy and waited around until the weather cleared, then got his sheep back on the trail and found his own camp.

For the remainder of his time in Wyoming, the thought of that cabin plagued him, and repeatedly, in his spare time, he searched the mountains for it, but never discovered it again. That was one of the big puzzles of his life.

"Pan made a better friend than he did a husband."
——Rebecca White

THOSE RESTLESS YEARS

Pan often frequented the local dances, held in different ranch houses. It was at one of these, that he met Caroline Hurtado, a pretty Indian girl. With his yen for the outdoors, and the western style of life, it was only natural he should fall in love with her. They were married by a Justice of the Peace in Lander, Wyoming; he was 19, she only 17.

Further down life's somewhat bumpy trail, Pan was to take two other women as his wife, but that was far into the future and all his thoughts at that time were for Caroline, his first love.

By the time of his marriage, Pan had acquired two saddle horses,which he put to double duty, after borrowing a wagon and harnesses. Caroline's father, Cal gave them permission to put a cabin on his ZZ Quarter Circle Ranch, near Crowheart, Wyoming, so Pan drove the team high up on the nearby mountain sides to cut,and haul in logs to begin construction.

At nineteen, he had filled out and become a muscular young man. The sweat flowed, the muscles rippled and the trees fell under his ax. The saddle horses took a dim view of the harness and wagon, but under Pan's tutouring, the material for the log cabin came off the mountain and it began to take shape.

One thing Pan never claimed to be was a carpenter; as a result the rough log home he built was classed as a shack, or a chicken coop, by many, including his young wife Caroline. "He put the windows in so high I couldn't even see out of them," she told us. Their furniture consisted of a rough board table, Pan had made, boxes for chairs, and a straw tick passed for a mattress. The stove, used both for cooking and heating the cabin, had also seen better days.

Things were rough, financially, in those days, during the depression, and any family was lucky just to have enough to eat. Pan and Caroline sometimes were down to living on the deer and antelope Pan hunted, for what little he earned on the ranches, only added up to coffee and bean money. Their meager food supply was augmented, gratefully, with milk and eggs given to them free, by Caroline's sister, Rebecca White, who lived nearby. Caroline was forced to make her own clothes and patch what limited apparel they had until there were more patches to be seen than the original fabric. On occassion, when there was a little extra money, Pan took advantage of it by joining in an elbow bending session with the boys, or a haircut, which he refused to forego.

With fond memories of good food, a good roof over his head, and a good bed, Pan decided he had enough cowboying and roughing it for a while, so in the fall of 1929, he decided to return, with Caroline, to Illinois. His family welcomed them with open arms and they stayed the winter at his parents' farm house; Pan helping his father with the chores. Caroline soon grew to love Pan's family, but still greatly missed her own family and friends in Wyoming.

By the spring of 1930, Pan was getting restless and as much to satisfy his itching feet as to get Caroline back to her family, he again bid his relatives goodbye, and returned to the log cabin at Crowheart. Two months later their first son, Homer, was born.

Pan went back to work as a top hand moving from one nearby ranch to another, not staying put at any one ranch for any length of time. Often, he joined his buddies on a 'toot' spending part of his wages for 'white lightning,' leaving little money for Caroline to buy food for her and by then, their two sons, Homer and Melvin.

Caroline had enough; she took the boys and left. Pan was completely shaken and painfully realized the errors of his ways in not being a good family provider. He went to Rebecca and tearfully asked her to intervene to get Caroline to come back to their home. But Rebecca didn't feel she could, or should, try to help in this way.

Since there seemed to be no hope of a reconciliation with Caroline, Pan's thoughts began to stray further west as he moved from ranch to ranch, cowboying, for the next couple of years, in the same general area of Wyoming. It was during this time he met Richmond Hobson, a greenhorn from the east, who was working at the Half Box E Ranch, trying to learn the cattle business. It seemed they were destined to meet, form a partnership as well as a lasting friendship, and ultimately become famous cattlemen.

PAN AND HIS PARTNER, Rich Hobson, are shown at "Wyoming Flats," after their arrival in the Chilcotin, with the Model "A" Ford panel that brought them into the country.

> "Pan never despaired. He was always looking ahead to the future."
>
> ——Veera Bonner

ON TO RAINBOW'S END

Pan had obtained a Canadian map showing a large area of unclaimed and undeveloped territory in Central British Columbia, and had studied it many nights by lamplight, when his daily riding was done. He began to tell Hobson about his discovery and in ensuing discussions between the two, he convinced Hobson that British Columbia held the chance of a lifetime for them. Then they began to consider immigrating to Canada, to try to get a ranch started somewhere in the area Pan had marked and remarked on the map. Pan was convinced that he had learned enough about cattle ranching in Wyoming to make it, and what he didn't know, he was prepared to bluff his way through.

Just one major problem existed. That was money, for he knew it would take more money than he had ever earned to get a cattle operation going. Hobson was in the same boat, so Pan relayed his enthusiasm to whoever would listen, in hope of getting someone else to throw in with them.

Daily, their plans and enthusiasm for the adventuresome project grew. Pan allowed that he could sell his team and wagon that he had by now acquired, the money to be spent on a car for the trip. He had obtained a Wyoming driver's license, but his driving experience was limited mostly to driving an old truck about the ranch. On the other hand, Hobson was a relatively experienced driver, so making the trek by car seemed the logical thing to do.

As their dreams began to jell into a plan of action, Hobson convinced Pan that he could raise money in the east to help fund the project, as long as they could find a suitable place for a ranch and prove to themselves and anyone else, that their plan was feasable.

Pan and Rich's ideas were the talk of the Wyoming ranching country and it wasn't too long before George Pennoyer, a successful rancher, told the two that if they could find a place in B.C. for a big spread and if it looked promising, he would throw in his share of money needed for an initial start. Pan and Rich were ecstatic.

Pan sold the team and wagon and made arrangements for the care of his saddle horses until he either came for them, or requested that they be sold. They were to remain behind on the Pennoyer Ranch. That last detail taken care of, there was nothing to hold him back.

They bought an old Model A Ford panel truck, that had been a meat wagon, loaded up their tack and personal gear and were ready to leave. Then came the hardest part of leaving for Pan. He stopped by to see his sons, for what might be the last time, in a long time, and to say "Goodbye" to Caroline. Even though they had not been living together the past few years, he still had a soft spot in his heart for her.

The first part of their trip was relatively uneventful, except for an occasional flat tire, the roads in the States being fair at that time, but after crossing the border, their first taste of wilderness roads came as they entered the hair raising Fraser Canyon, in British Columbia. The old road fairly hung over the raging waters hundreds of feet below. Many places were one way only and the two lane sections allowed very little room to pass another vehicle. Coming from the relatively flat lands of Wyoming, the canyon trip was a thrill a minute for them.

Then came the grueling drive west from Williams Lake, to their proposed destination, Anahim Lake. It took many days, progressing from one mud hole to another, each creating back breaking labour to get the old Ford unstuck and on the way to the next bog. There is little doubt but what they could have made much better time with a team and wagon.

Pan and Rich's first view of the town (if you could call it that) was one that would gladden the heart of very few. It consisted of log cabins, buildings and sheds in various states of disrepair, scattered about in no symmetrical pattern, no sidewalks or streets, just dusty wagon trails. Part of the town consisted of the Indian reserve settlement and it too was a scattering of cabins with the church and school house being the predominant buildings, the only ones showing signs of maintenance.

Teams and wagons were in evidence and saddled horses were tied to various hitching posts. There wasn't another car in sight and from the horses' reactions as they passed, Pan felt sure they had been exposed to very few vehicles. It was just as he had dreamed it would be, as if the clock had been turned back fifty years.

"Pan adhered to the code of the old west which still
prevailed in the Chilcotin. One thing you didn't do was
to ask a person about his past."

——Dude Lavington

EUREKA! THE PROMISED LAND

Pan and Rich's arrival in the Chilcotin, and Anahim
Lake in particular, was ill timed. It was the fall, of 1934,
and winter was on the doorstep, leaving no time to scout
the land before the snows came. There was little they could
accomplish in locating their dream ranch; they could only
dig in for the coming freeze-up.

By making a few initial inquires of the local
residents, they were directed to a small meadow where
they could get in with the Ford panel. Under Pan's
'uncapable' directions, they began to put up a cabin,using
logs from a stand of jackpines nearby. The cabin went up
quickly, for Pan allowed that it would take much less time
if they didn't bother to notch the logs too deep. After the
walls were up, he figured then they could use moss,
swamp grass and mud to chink them with.

Their stove, stove pipe, door hinges, windows and
furnishings were as makeshift as the construction. The
end result was the cabin being classed as another 'hen
house' by the locals, who had watched their progress.
There were many reservations as to its 'winterbility.'

Alfred Bryant, a local rancher's son, came in over the
mountains from Bella Coola, with a load of freight on his
pack outfit, and the first thing his father, Lord Cyrus
Bryant, told him was that a couple of "Pilgrims" had come
into the country and put up a shack down on Goose Flats,
(which later became known as Wyoming Flats and carries
that name to this day).

Alfred was curious, so took a look and reported, "It's
damn near cold enough already to freeze the balls off a
brass monkey down there. Those God damn Americans
will freeze to death in that 'pecker pole' shack." Alfred
used the explicit language of the Chilcotin Country.

"You're right," Cyrus agreed. "One's a city dude and
the other's a Wyoming ranch hand and they don't know
better, I guess. I'd better go rescue them first chance I
get."

When Alfred got back from his next pack trip, he found Pan and Rich at Bryant's Ranch, happy to have a warm spot to lay out their bedrolls. As well, Alfred noted, they were not hesitant to do more than their share of the chores around the ranch.

Pan and Rich took advantage of any loose time to ride around visiting other ranches and grew to know the Smiths, Christensens, Holtes, and Dorseys plus several Indian families. Pan, also used the opportunity to seek out their unique ways of ranching in this totally different country, that he knew little of. There were many home brew parties and their new friends discovered Pan was no slouch when it came to putting away the suds, running a close second only to Hobson. It was at these social times that several of Pan's personality traits became apparent too. One was of his ability not only to conjure up situations, but to take advantage of every unplanned opportunity to play a prank on anyone, any age, or any sex.

His sister, Ada Irene, told of this one that he pulled throughout his adult lifetime. "One of the times he was home, in Illinois, Pan pulled his trick of smoking a cigarette without shaking the ashes off. I was certainly hurrying around to find him an ashtray. He always was quite a teaser."

One family that Pan favoured with his visits, maybe more than others, was the Holtes, who had immigrated from Spokane, Washington, some years before. They happened to have two good-looking daughters, Alyce and Ila. Of course, Pan passed his visits off as a chance to visit with the boys, Tom and Jimmy, and parents Andy and Hattie, but the open admiration shown by the girls didn't escape him. He soaked it up like sun on a winter's day.

Pan and Alfred Bryant soon became close friends too, and Pan found himself traveling about more with Alfred than with Rich. On one occasion they made the long, hard ride across the mountains to the Maxwell Ranch at Chezacut, to look at cattle, with the view to buying some later on.

Many hours were spent, by Pan and Rich the two would-be cattlemen, around the big pot-bellied heater in the Dorsey home visiting, but also laying out plans for building a ranch house, once they had found Pan's dream range. Lester Dorsey and his wife Mickey, were as excited as Pan and Rich, with Lester promising to build better log buildings than Pan knew existed, when the time came.

In February, the Bryants moved to a 10' by 12' cabin at their winter hay feeding camp, and since Pan and Rich's 'guesting' would have crowded them, the boys moved to Christensen's "big meadow camp" and spent the rest of the winter in a small log cabin there, built to withstand the unpredictable weather yet to come.

In the spring, as the snow at the lower elevations began to melt, Pan's excitement for the adventure that lay ahead, grew by leaps and bounds. On every clear day, he could be seen staring at the still snow clad Ilgachuz Mountains to the north and the Itchas to the northeast. He tried desperately to picture in his mind, the land beyond his vision, the land that lay on the other side of the peaks.

It was time to make more definite plans, so Pan and Rich began to use their time more constructively. They spent what was left of their Wyoming stake to buy horses, tack and supplies, in preparation for their trek into the little known Blackwater country.

Pan's bubbling enthusiasm had rubbed off on the Holtes. Tommy had once been over the mountains, and agreed to guide them into the area. His father, Andy, just couldn't watch them ride off on such an adventure and agreed to join in with them, part way.

The maps available then were of no use to them as they only had the approximate positions of the mountains, with few of the details, such as streams and lakes, indicated. Only by word of the trappers and Indians had Pan and Rich been able to get a hint of what the country had in store for them.

They began their journey on a frosty spring morning, their guide was 18 year old, Tommy Holte; their pack train a mixture of trained and 'green' horses; and their excitement at its peak, or so they believed.

Tommy Holte told us, "The trip up the mountain side was fairly easy, compared to what we encountered going **around into the Blackwater. We climbed to a point, where we could look out over the country to the north, in only three days, after leaving the meadows near Anahim Lake. Dad (Andy Holte) helped us through the lower bog country, and once we got higher in elevation, the ground became drier and the traveling easier for us all. When we reached the place from where we could see those big,** wild, grass meadows, Pan and Rich were beside themselves with excitement - it looked like the promised land Pan had been seeking.

That excitement nearly killed them later. The four men had come back off the mountain, then Pan, Rich and Tommy had set out on the old, northbound Indian trail, following the west side of the Ilgachuz, until they thought they could ride directly east, through the jackpines, to the meadows, without any problems.

Their goal was a giant meadow, one much larger in area than all the rest, one they had made out clearly from the mountain top. They had made a rough sketch of the country below, too, but at that height the bogs and marshes were not visible. Andy had warned them of these dangerous pitfalls, but in their rush in making their own trail, they forgot his warning and got lost in a huge marshland, nearly losing their horses and supplies. However, Pan was cool-headed and an excellent horse-man, as so many of his friends have attested to, and was able to get them through and pointed in the right direction again, that time at a more careful pace.

The three reached the meadow days later, exhausted and mosquito bitten. When they came out into the open grass, Pan was speechless, he couldn't believe his eyes. The natural grass in the meadow was already knee high and thick enough to support many cattle.

They sat for a few moments, trying to comprehend that they had actually found the land they had been searching for. But night would soon be on them so they hurried to set up a camp along the river bank. They settled in for about a week, exploring each day, discovering meadow after meadow with enough grass to feed hundreds of cows. It was more than Pan had dared to dream of and in his estimation, it held the promise of becoming a rival to the famed Cariboo Gang Ranch.

Their supplies low, they started out, back to Anahim Lake. This time they blazed the trail from "their meadows" to where they again intersected the Indian trail. Next time it would be easier to return. At the Holte's it took little salesmanship to talk Tom and Andy into going back to begin construction of the first log cabin, as per Pan's instructions, near where they had camped.

Pan and Rich continued on into Anahim Lake where Pan used one of the few phones to call Pennoyer, in

Wyoming. Excitedly, he told him they had located "some
of the greatest cattle grazing land in the world." He asked
Pennoyer to sell his saddle horses for him and wire the
money so they could get on with their plans. Pennoyer
agreed to take care of it immediately, which he did.

"Pan had a terrific sense of concentration."

——Toby Cave

THE IMMIGRANT

With the ranch site discovered and his bank roll somewhat replenished, Pan was getting edgy to get on with his plans. His visitor's permit was about to expire, so he began to lay plans for a trip to Vancouver to pick up the necessary settler's effects, that were required, and to advise Canadian Immigration officials of his decision to become a landed immigrant.

Rich and he had spent hours making out a rough drawing of the range areas and meadows they had explored, and had it well identified, as to location, in reference to the mountains. While down in the lower mainland, they planned to take the ferry over to Victoria, there they would file an application for Pre-emption on as much land as possible, plus they wanted to discuss grazing rights on additional acres, with the Lands Department.

Pan and Rich, after much discussion, talked Alfred Bryant into accompanying them on the trip, as he had the know how to help in selecting the right tools they would need to develop the ranch. Tents, kitchen ware, axes, cross cut saws, hammers, nails, whip saws, and tack topped the seemingly endless list.

Since Alfred had never been to the city, he jumped at the chance to go with them. The trio was soon on the way in the less-than-trusty Ford Panel; the trip ahead to Williams Lake a long hard two hundred miles of ruts and holes that could bury a moose, standing up, in. The first leg was to Alexis Creek, and by the time they got there, the spring thaws had begun to soften the road during the day, so they cooled their heels until the evening frost hit again and the road hardened up, then another long day of fighting mud and ruts brought them into Williams Lake.

When they had left Anahim Lake, they were all reasonably clean in buckskin jackets and jeans, but by the time they hit Williams Lake, their clothes were so muddy they would stand in the corner by themselves. Also the tires on the panel were about shot. However, they hurried on.

At Ashcroft, 125 miles further down the highway, they found one used tire to fit the rig and continued on the cliff-hanging journey down the Fraser. In Chilliwack another tire was purchased and they drove on into Vancouver in fair, but grubby, style. Alfred ogled the tall buildings, street cars, the snarl of traffic, and the well dressed ladies. Pan put up a good front, acting as though he was used to the cities, but when he walked into the Georgia Hotel to register, Alfred began to doubt Pan had ever been in such a classy place before, after noticing his expression as he took in the lobby grandeur. And he was right. It was the first time Pan had ever played the big spender and stayed in such luxurious accomodations, then only because Hobson had insisted on it.

Meantime the doorman, resplendent in his fancy uniform, was eyeing the mud coated ex-sausage truck, they had left parked at the front door. Noticing his intrest, Pan bellowed from the door, "Park that there rig for us, will ya?" Alfred stepped behind Pan, anticipating the action, knowing full well that Pan had baited the doorman.

Before climbing in, the doorman noted the muddy front seat, so he acquired a rag and meticulously cleaned it off. then once behind the wheel, found that the truck wouldn't start.

Another bellow from Pan, "You'll have to crank her. Battery's dead."

Disgustedly, the doorman set the brake, set the spark and throttle, and climbed back out to hand crank it. The old crate came to life, after three vigorous twists, but loose motor mounts had put a bind on the crank handle and it wouldn't come out. The doorman jumped back, nearly doing a pratt fall in the street, to escape the crank spinning like a meat grinder gone berserk. Pan watched, grinning like a jackass eating thistles, and Alfred bent double, laughing.

However, the doorman, his composure somewhat shaken, got into the truck, drove it around to the parking lot with the crank still whirling, and returned to his station, no doubt hoping for a big tip. But Pan and Alfred had fled the scene and were on their way up to their room. Rich had missed the whole fiasco, he had managed to find the nearest bar.

Other passengers, in the elevator, keep eyeballing Pan and Alfred in their muddy buckskins, with their old scuffed suitcase bound around the middle by a man's tie to keep it from popping open. Pan had crammed Alfred's clothes in his suitcase and it had been just a bit more than the old case could stand, so it had popped a few seams. Not knowing what else to do, Pan and Alfred smiled, nodded and acted nonchalant.

The next three days were busy ones, what with getting squared away on their entry forms with the Immigration people and, in Victoria, getting the paper work started on the ranch land. As could be expected some time was taken off for a few belts in the local pubs. Alfred kept forgetting himself and spitting on the sidewalk, for which he caught hell from Pan. "You've gotta remember where you are and act like you're civilized even if you ain't," Pan admonished his friend.

Finally, with the truck so loaded it was setting on the axles, they set out north. From Vancouver to Alexis Creek was not uneventful, as far as road problems go, but they managed to make it without breaking down in the overloaded vehicle.

While there overnight, Pan loked over a string of horses for sale and began dickering. Now Pan considered himself a fair man, there was little argument on that point - except when it came to horseflesh, then he looked at the whole business of trading as open domain for any deal he could make. This was to be no exception. But by early the next afternoon, Alfred and he were astride two good saddle horses, two more in tow, and two colts necked together following. Hobson was ahead of them in the panel. Pan never did let Alfred in on the horse buying details, since he wasn't one to disclose his affairs either about his horse trading deals or with the opposite gender, but he sure was curious as Pan chuckled and sported a secretive smile for the first mile or so down the road.

After prying and pushing and pulling the Ford out of several mud holes, the whole procession made it to Redstone, where once again Pan made a deal on several horses, while Rich and Alfred laid back at their campfire.

At Kleena Kleene Pete McCormack took a shine to the model A and another trade was made. By this time the string of horses was quite impressive; for Pan, everything was right with the world.

The next few hours work, however, was not as easy as the deal making had been for they had to cut out several horses to use as packers,then initiate the new pack saddles by transfering the load from the panel to them. Anxious to be on his way, Pan prodded Alfred and Rich saying, "Quit yer horsing around. We got places to get to."

It wasn't an easy ride out of Kleena Kleene, as the new horses fought against leaving their home pastures and the packs, but the three adventurers agreed they would like to detour, from the main road, and go into George Power's ranch on Charlotte Lake, even if it did mean riding out of their way. George had extened a sincere invitation, not that one was needed in the Chilcotin, to "drop in anytime," when he had previously met Pan and Rich in Anahim Lake. Besides, they reasoned in unison, it was another chance to see more of the country, to possibly pick up a few more tricks of ranching there, and a few days rest seemed in order after their trip to Vancouver, Pan forgetting his earlier haste.

They took the trail cut off just short of Towdystan, on the way into Powers Ranch. This brought up the subject of the famed stop which Pan had asked Alfred about on the way out in the Ford. He was intrigued by the place, so he suggested to Rich and Alfred that they stop there on their way to Anahim Lake, after visiting Powers, to get acquainted, which they did.

There they met Fred Engebretson, who's grandfather Jacob Lunos, had built the ranch in 1899, then turned it over to the Engebretson family, including sons Harold and Fred, when he could no longer run it. Almost from the first, it was a logical stopover for travelers from Williams Lake to Anahim Lake and Bella Coola. Pan hardly ever passed it by again.

Fred remembers Pan's visits well. "Pan would either bring news or ask what was going on. When he came in from Williams Lake, it was just like getting a newspaper."

Pan relished the 'bull sessions' around the stove in the evenings. He reveled in the fact that he was staying at the same place where the Dalton brothers, Emmett and George, met and stayed in their 1915 sojourn into British Columbia. Pan liked to relive, in his mind, the stories of the old, old, west.

In 1926, Powers had built a blacksmith shop at Towdystan, (which means liquor in Indian) and Pan had work done in the old shop from time to time after the first visit.

Meals and lodging, in the days of Pan's early stopovers, were 50¢; stabling a horse was another 50¢ per night, but there was no charge for letting a mount run in the pasture. Initials carved in the old bunk house log walls, date back to 1901 and were many. Apparently, Pan had too much talking to do, for he never took the time to add his initials with the rest, at least we could not find them there. The only records of his visits are forged in Fred's keen mind.

From Towdystan, they trailed out to Anahim Lake and then into the Home Ranch — the name Pan and Rich had chosen for their new home while sitting beside one of their roadside campfires.

Pan was now a Canadian settler, officially and spiritually.

"Pan was so tough he could wipe his ass with a handfull
of thistles, yet not too proud to shed a tear for the
passing of a friend."

——Bill Solowoniuk

LOOKING AHEAD

For the next thirty five years, Pan's whole life revolved
around the Home Ranch, where four of his children, one by
his second wife, Adelia (Shorty) and three by Betty, his
third wife, spent part of their lives.

In ensuing chapters, we will try and give you a look into
Pan's life during those thirty five years and into the
following years, after he established his fishing camp. Of
necessity these shall be only the highlites, for space does
not permit a day by day discourse of his activities spanning
that much time. Pan's life being far from the normal
rancher's life.

At first Pan and Rich Hobson lived in the cabin, built
by Andy and Tommy Holt, along with the 'hands' like Alfred
Bryant, who first worked for them the summer of 1935,
before going back to freighting. Then in 1937, Lester
Dorsey was hired to build the main ranch house. In the
interim, corrals, a barn, tool shed, blacksmith shop,
outhouse and a food cache had been put up. Later on,
another log struture became the Home Ranch Store.

The partnership between Pan and Rich had evolved
into the Frontier Cattle Company, after the second summer
when Rich went to New York to raise funds while Pan
made a quick hospital trip to have his appendix removed.
Grant Noble, the only hired hand at the time, stayed on to
watch the ranch. As a result of Hobson's trip, Alan
Stuyvesant and associates in New York and George
Pennoyer of Wyoming became the company's backers.

As remote as it was there seemed to be a never ending
stream of 'pilgrims' passing by the Home Ranch. Before
the war, during the last stages of the depression, there was
a steady string of hardy individuals making the long trek
over, or around, the Ilgachuz mountains into the
Blackwater looking for work. Word of the Frontier Cattle
Company's existence, and its vast land holdings and

reportedly huge cattle herds had spread far and wide. To some it sounded like a utopia. A few landed jobs, while others got only a free meal and were sent on their way.

Ranching history was made there, when Pan thought out and Lester Dorsey drew up the plans, then constructed a giant, wood harrow to be used in taming the wild meadows. It took sixteen horses to pull the finished machine, with an excellent teamster on the reins. Lester made the initial swath, brought it back to the cabin, did some adjustments and turned it over to Pan.

Packing in the metal parts for the harrow, and all the other machinery necessary, by horses from Bella Coola, was only part of the daily ranch life. Clearing the land, felling trees for the miles of fences and corrals, with all the attending hardships, is a story that has been told and retold in the Chilcotin and Blackwater through the years.

On December 11, 1937, a story appeared in the Vanderhoof Nechako Chronical that told of the "Cornstock (we believed it to be Comstock) Batnuni Ranch" sale to the Frontier Cattle Company. At that time, Rich Hobson took over as forman there and Pan became the Home Ranch foreman.George Pennoyer came north fromWyoming to act as General Manager. Thus Pan was harnessed to the Home Ranch operation for the duration of the company's existance.

In 1941, Pennoyer was forced to return to Wyoming because of ill health and full management responsibilities then rested on Pan and Rich's shoulders.

During those first five years, Pan led an unbelievable life. Remember- it was just before the war years, and not in the 1800s that most of us associate pioneering with. How many men today would think of going out in 40 degree below zero wheather, saddling up a horse and plodding off on a 200 mile ride, knowing they had to sleep out under a tree on the trail every night? Knowing that they had to face blowing snow, drifts, icy creeks and bitter cold ?

How many could face the loneliness that Pan Phillips did ? Days on end of either riding along alone, or sitting on a wagon seat, watching the endless miles of rocks, bogs, and logs roll under the wheels, through the long line of jackpines that blocked out all view, except straight up? What must have gone through his mind ?

It seems to us that Pan thrived on a life that would

have beaten any lesser man.

If the day to day intracacies, misfortunes and adventures of cattle ranching interests you, both Rich Hobson and Pan's friend Dude Lavington have written books covering the subjects in great detail.

Hobson wrote, Grass Beyond the Mountains, Nothing Too Good For A Cowboy, and Rancher Takes a Wife. Lavington authored, The Nine Lives Of A Cowboy and Born To Be Hung. All five books covered Blackwater ranching in more detail than we can go into in this biography, and Pan's life and escapades play some part of each.

As a result of Hobson's books, which were well written and fired the imagination, other writers took up the cry and Pan's fame spread. Innumerable articles have been published about him and as a result many claim that "Pan Phillips became a myth. Some thought he could walk on water."

No matter what he did, no matter how insignificant it may have been, word would spread and another morsel of folklore was added to his legend. "Knowing Pan became a status symbol." especially after the 1969 CBC television show about his cattle drive to Quesnel (details in a later chapter).

There are those who claim that Pan's life, as a rancher, was no different than anyone else's, but we do believe the facts we have laid out will prove he stood a head taller than the average. Read on , then you be the judge.

"Pan -- he damn good man with team."

————Antoine Baptiste

FREIGHTING

Freighting played a major role in Pan's life. He spent many hours and days, reins tightly held in his hands, under some of the most adverse conditions imaginable.

Today, when the word freighting is mentioned, we think of railroads, semi-trucks and even jet aircraft, but in Pan's freighting days it meant packhorses, wagons or sleighs pulled by two horses (they occasionally used 4 up, or 6 up) and later on, a half-track tractor.

When the ranch was first started, all supplies were brought in by pack train, from Anahim Lake, but Pan did make a few trips to pick up special orders, from the Union Steamship Company, in Bella Coola. He brought the first heavy equipment, mower, rake, etc., by that long trek over and back, in all approximately 300 miles, with a pack train, the horses carrying loads that set records for weight, per horse; records which are still talked about around the trail camp fires.

Driving the Bella Coola road today, you would hardly believe that men and horses found their way over the rough terrain, but the pack trail followed a much easier route than the road does. In fact, it was a gentle enough slope that if the packer took his time, the horses could keep moving right along, up and around the one switchback, into Sugar Creek valley, then on up across through the pass and down into Anahim Lake; stopping only for lunches and nightfall. The trip usually was made in three days.

If the supplies (freight) were picked up at Stan Dowling's store in Anahim Lake, the first stop on the way into the ranch, would be at Christensens, next the Holtes, Peter Alexis' and home. If Pan reached any of the in-between places too late to continue on, he would stay the night, carrying all his freezeable supplies into the house or bunkhouse, where they could be kept warm by the stove. It was tiring work, but no one ever heard Pan grumble, he took it all in stride as part of his chosen way of life. Once when the mercury stood at 50 degrees below (F) he was heard to say, "The box of apples I brought in by the fire, cooked on one side and froze on the other."

At that time, with Rich buying supplies in Vanderhoof and Pan in Anahim Lake for the F.C.C., George began to figure they should merge their buying power to save money by buying in quantity and he set up a meeting between Pan, Hobson and himself in Quesnel.

As usual, on arrival in town, they set up headquarters in the Quesnel Hotel (this was before they adopted the Log Cabin Court as the scene of their activities) and began mixing business with pleasure, the liquid kind. Word got around town that there were three 'rich' Americans at the hotel, on a spending spree for the new F.C.C. The news finally trickled into the office of John A. Fraser Company, Ltd., a general merchandising firm that sold everything from soup to nuts, literally, plus harness, cow bells, washboards, feed, clothes and 'you name it' items.

Alex Fraser was working for his father, John, then and after hearing the news, he strode down to the hotel, found the room and introduced himself to the three head honchos, Pan, Rich and George. After a few empties had hit the waste basket, a friendship developed, they all relaxed and Alex began talking prices. It was apparent that Fraser had come with a sharp pencil and wanted their business. The trio liked the way he shot prices from the hip, so a deal was struck then and there; the F.C.C. would buy all their supplies from Fraser's store, even though it meant a longer haul for Pan. Alex was a happy young man that October day, for the initial order was equivalent to all the business the store had done so far that year.

Pan's subsequent orders, loaded on a freight rig, either the wagon or a sleigh, were for basic staples, like flour, sugar, lard, bacon, beans, rice, macaroni, canned milk, etc.; however, the freight rigs leaving for the Batnuni Ranch were carrying food more along the gourmet line, like jelly, candy, nuts, baking chocolate, canned fruits, and all the other good things you can imagine in the cupboard.

About the second time Pan sat in on the settlement with Frasers, it became apparent to him that Rich and his crew were living high on the hog, New York style, while he and his crew were eating beans and blowing off steam. Pan, reportedly, blew more steam than usual at that meeting, for the grocery bills leveled out a bit after that.

Pan continued trading with Fraser's store, even after the F.C.C. was disbanded, but then went on to dividing his trips between Anahim Lake and Quesnel.

On one of his winter trips into Quesnel, Pan took a young man named David Stirling, who had come by the ranch looking for a job after being sent west by his family, through connections with the backers of the F.C.C. Young Stirling arrived, all 6 ft., 180 lbs. of him, with a chip on his shoulder, afraid of nothing. Somehow he was sure, there was not much to learn about cattle or horses, that it would not take him much time, so after a few weeks, he began to lay plans to make a ride across B.C. from the Blackwater to Banff, then across the rest of Canada, climbing a 'few' mountains enroute. An ambitious project to say the least.

Pan took over the task of trying to teach him something of ranch work and in time Stirling became known as the "Six month wonder," for there didn't seem to be much that he thought he didn't know about horses, cattle, ranching, and so on and on, by the end of that time.

Pan was noncommittal about Stirling, but the rest of the hands were convinced that he was fast becoming a burr under Pan's saddle blanket and surmised there would come a day when Pan would make up for it.

They were right. It was on a winter freight trip that Pan took David along to help. He had four sleighs to haul provisions, from Quesnel, into the Home Ranch both for his store and their daily supplies. That meant caring for sixteen head of horses along the trail. As usual hay had been left at each spot they planned to stop overnight on the return trip. Stirling carried his own weight when it came to handling a pitchfork, so Pan never had to put the spurs to him there.

In town they had the usual blowout and when the party was over thoughts of loading the sleighs and heading back were met head on with unforseen trouble. A chinook wind had melted the snow for several miles west of town. With five tons of flour, sugar, grain and other foodstuffs, it was a serious problem. Alex Fraser solved the first part by trucking the freight out about six miles, from town to the snow line, until he could go no further with the truck. Once loaded, the sleighs moved down the road until they again hit a patch of road where the sun had melted the snow off the gravel. For about a half mile even with two teams hitched to a sleigh, it became apparent there was no way the horses could move the load on the bare road. So it was obvious to Pan that he would have to unload, then take all four empty sleighs above the next snow line, and reload, carrying all 150 sacks up the hill. Each sack weighed out differently, some 50 lbs., some 100 lbs., some 200 lbs.

It was back breaking work and it didn't take Pan's helpers long to figure out why it wasn't bothering him too much, he seemed to be enjoying having to face the problem head on. In his figuring as how to get the freight across the bare road, he had also figured how he could avoid the hard work and that was by staying at the bottom of the hill, doling out the sacks. To each man Pan either handed two 50 pound sacks, one for under each arm; or one 100 pound sack they could carry over their shoulder.

But when it came Stirling's turn, Pan reached for the 200 pound sacks, using all his strength and controlling his facial muscles so to Stirling it looked as if he was tossing about the lighter ones. For any problems David had presented Pan during the previous months, Pan received payment that day as he watched the man struggle under his heavy load time after time all the while trying to act like it was nothing at all. Pan never did figure out if David ever got wise to the differences in weights; if he did, Stirling never let on.

David Stirling went on to become a famous World War II hero, fighting with Montgomery, in the desert, against Rommel. Perhaps some of the things he learned from Pan Phillips, out in the Blackwater, stood him in good stead over there.

Pan had his share of weather related problems in freighting. Another time he was leaving Nazko with a loaded sleigh, when the weather began to warm up. By the time he was a half day out of Kluskus, the snow had become so soft it was nearly impossible for the team to keep the sleigh moving, as the horses kept breaking through the crust, followed by the heavy rig.

Pan was pondering the situation, when Paul Krestenuk, who had been a general freighter in the Blackwater for many years, met him about an hour out of Kluskus. Paul was going out empty so he hadn't had any problem. They stopped to chat by a quickly made fire and a can of 'sugar stop tea.' Pan said he knew he would never make it to the ranch, still a four day trip, at least, with the trail conditions as they were. So he asked Paul where he might store some of his supplies to lighten his load, without losing them to 'sticky fingers,' before he could get back with pack horses or a wagon to get them.

Paul suggested the church, the only substansial building left from the time when Kluskus had a population of 4,000 people, which by then had dwindled to a handful. Pan followed his advice. The horses then pulled the lightened sleigh easily on into the ranch. But Pan spent many anxious weeks, during the breakup, worrying about his supplies, and if they would still be there, for they represented many hard-to-come-by dollars. When he finally did return to Kluskus, he found everything just as he had left it. What he hadn't fully realized, the Indians, too, were basically honest people in those days.

On an early fall trip, the snows came long before Pan had anticipated. It was so deep, in no way could the horses pull the wagon through. He had to leave it, so he unhitched the team, rode one horse and led the other home. After warming up and getting prepared the next day, Pan returned to the snowbound wagon with pack horses, transfered the load to them and left the wagon there.

The next spring, after breakup, Pan and Rex Bartlett, a friend in from the States on holidays, rode the horses back to the wagon. They hitched up and went back into Anahim Lake, via the Bill Lehman ranch.

The streams were still flooded, so both arrived at Bill's ranch soaking wet. Jane Lehman (nee Bryant), Bill's wife, took one look, put the water on for tea and Mike, their son, dug out some dry clothes for them. Jane hung theirs to dry over the usual drying rack above the kitchen range and they settled in for the night. After breakfast the next morning, Pan and Rex continued on to Anahim Lake. Rex recalled Pan's remark as they left Lehmans, "Now you know, Rex, what Chilcotin hospitality is all about."

After the trail was slashed to Anahim Lake in the pass between the Ilgachuz and the Itcha Mountains, in 1941, Pan used wagons and sleighs entirely, allowing him to haul bigger loads at a time, with less physical effort on his part. The mountain trail, however, couldn't be used during the worst of the winter's snowfalls.

When Pan left the ranch, he usually took a load of hay,

stashing it along the way to use for feed on the return trip.
This was an absolute necessity on the winter runs. He
made these his regular night stops during the years, and
was as much at home sitting alongside the campfire as he
was in the house.

His trips over the mountain only took two days,
compared to the three or more around the mountain, but if
the weather did not cooperate, they might take four or
more. If caught on the trail in below zero weather, it meant
keeping hot rocks, or a lighted coal oil lantern under the
tarp, covering his load, to keep his supplies from freezing.
The horses were tethered close to the fire, covered with a
blanket and fed grain, for warmth.

Springtimes, Pan tried to time his day's drive so he
would be setting up camp at Tsilbekue Creek before
nightfall. The creek, at that time of year, would be running
full of trout, spawners drawn back to their natural grounds
in the gravel beds along the banks. There was no need for
fishing tackle, or even a net. Pan merely followed the bear's
system, wading into the stream, submerging his cupped
hands under the water's surface, then tossing onto shore
the first good solid male fish that swam by. Sometimes it
was a contest though, as to which one would win, Pan
splashing out of the water to grab his catch, or the fish
flopping back into the water to escape the frying pan.
Supper that night would be fried trout, and Pan always ate
his fill.

For the reader, it may be hard to picture yourself
sitting in Pan's place on the wagon seat, on a trip, jolting
and twisting, over a hundred miles of rocks, bogs and tree
stumps strewn on the way in front of you. The sleigh was an
easier ride, for then some of the roughness was covered
and it would glide across the frozen bogs and lakes with
ease. But, then too, there was the cold.

Having traveled the trail, from Nazko to the Home
Ranch, ourselves, let us describe it as it was, from Pan's
point of view--looking up a horse's patutti.

First by sleigh. Pan would wake up before first light,
the slicker over his bedroll covered with six inches of snow.
The camp fire would be only a glow or else completely out.
First, he would re-kindle the fire and put on water to heat
for tea. Then he plowed through the snow towards the
horses, oat pails in hand, to feed them. Usually, he tied the

horses under a tree to protect them and the hay. Their backs would be covered with snow, and they would whinney when he approached.

After 'graining' them, he would shake the harness free of snow and hitch the team to the sleigh. Then his breakfast would be a cup of hot tea, jerky and bannock. Before he pulled on his gloves, he gave his hands a last warming over the fire. If the weather was not yet cold enough to force him under the canvas, he climbed on the seat; ready to start another day of traveling.

From the first snap of the reins, Pan had to be alert. His only references as to where the trail ran, would be the blazed trees. The drifting snow, white outs, and frost covered trees, made it nearly impossible to recognize the main route. He had to keep his eyes ahead watching for the tell tale blaze on a tree, or the opening in the pines that indicated the trail lay beneath the snow.

Not long after he started, he saw the ice forming on the horses' fetlocks; next the top of their tails became frosty; soon ice crystals spread along their back; then their chin whiskers would ice up; followed by frost on the long hair on their withers, legs and tails. In the meantime, Pan had as little as possible of his face exposed to the wind; once in a while he had to reach up to break the ice off his upper lip. In that cold, there is no way a person can stop their nose from running, once the tap gets turned on. Undoubtedly, Pan spent more comfortable hours, elsewhere, than on the seat of a sleigh.

It was a peaceful ride though, with the swish of the runners breaking through the crusty snow, the muted jingle of harness chains, an occasional fart, or snort, from the team, and the creak of the sleigh bedboards, as the only sounds, and they were muffled by the snow. Pan must have felt, many times, he was the only person on earth.

At the first creek crossing, he would halt the team, grab his axe and cut a hole in the ice for the horses to get water. Patiently, he would then try to urge them across the slick ice, without falling and cracking the sleigh tongue, breaking their harness, or hurting themselves. Where the dense patches of jackpine crowded the trail, he had to be especially careful, for if he hung up a runner and broke it, he could have serious problems.

Second by wagon: Pan faced different problems in the summer time. The trip was much longer for he had to go around, rather than across a marsh or up an ice covered lake. Rivers and streams were running fuller and swifter, and often he had to clear downed timber from across the trail. However the days were longer.

Pan's first wagon in the Blackwater was an iron wheeled one, the box and seat made out of rough lumber, produced from a local saw mill. It was truly a rough ride and created many sore bums and aching joints. Then he bought a 'Bennett Buggy,' which was made from the frame, axles wheels and tires of a wrecked vehicle; a box being built on top. But it was the tires that made the difference. Being rubber they absorbed the jolts somewhat and cushioned the ride. With the addition of a folded bear hide on the seat, Pan's ride then became bearable. (No pun intended.)

On steep downgrades, the Bennett buggy he used, had no brakes so there would be a point where the team could no longer hold back, bracing themselves against the loaded, rolling wagon. They then would try to out run it. The team still responded to the reins, but at a full gallop on the twisty trail. If Pan didn't guide them with the utmost skill, they could hook a wheel on a tree, or stump, and his whole day would have been ruined. Or if he let the wagon hit a large rock, he was apt to unload himself along with half his freight.

On the level, where the trail was free of rocks and fairly smooth, Pan would always get a thrill watching his horses in full run, emphasized by the trace chains, jingling up a rhythm in their unison of movement.

Each animal had a disposition of it's own and Pan knew his teams; their reactions to his commands, a rifle shot, a grouse flying up at their feet, a bear in the trail ahead; or any one of a number of other things that might turn up. Knowing them so well, kept Pan one jump ahead of their reactions.

Pan had one old horse that wasn't always raring to go, unless of course they were a half day out from the Home Ranch. Then if Pan stopped the team to rest, that horse would turn it's head, look straight down the wagon tongue and stare him in the eye, as if to ask why in hell they had stopped, since the home pastures were such a short distance away.

Once in a while Pan would hitch up a team that had a stubborn streak. From then on the day wouldn't go right, for if he came to a creek crossing where the bank looked slick, or something in the water spooked them, they would balk. At that point Pan didn't dare let the horses win. If he absolutely could not get them to go ahead, he would turn the wagon tail to the stream, and back across, outsmarting the team.

After many lonely hours, by himself, meditating, Pan would be overjoyed to meet another wagon or have a rider overtake him. That usually called for a 'sugar stop tea' break, summer or winter. It was considered a real treat by the Indians, and after a short, friendly bull session each would go on their way again. Perhaps the day being a bit brighter after meeting a friendly face.

Pan thought he was prepared for any unexpected occurence on his many trips, but one winter day, out on the sleigh, about thirty miles from home he got a shock. Bundled up against the 35 degrees below zero cold, he heard a rifle shot and a bullet splattered into a tree beside him, just missing his head. Reacting quickly, he jumped from the seat, reins in his hands, and urged the team into a trot, using the sleigh as a shield. He didn't think he had an enemy in the world so the ambush was quite uncomprehensive to him. Once he felt he was in the clear, he hopped back onto the sleigh and kept moving as fast as possible until he was well out of range.

"Jesus Christ! That guy shot pretty close!" Pan excitedly told the crew when he got home.

Pan soon found out who had taken the shot at him and why. It was another settler in the Blackwater, with a bad case of cabin fever who had apparently gone amuck. Pan had tried to help him before, and needless to say, not being a quitter, continued to be the man's friend. The chap ultimately recovered his senses so we will not reveal his name as Pan wouldn't have wanted us to. When any of his friends had problems, Pan suffered with them, and such was the case here.

There were some places along the trail where Pan could tie the reins up, catch a cat nap, or take out the makings and roll himself a smoke, and leave the driving to the horses. Usually, where the trail was extra wide or when crossing a large meadow, the horses knew the way without guidance, and Pan would give his arms a rest.

The acquistion of a tractor, in the mid 1950s, made Pan's freighting easier still. He not only brought in his supplies, but with the addition of a half track on the tractor for winter's use, he was able to earn extra cash by hauling for others, including Tascha Lake Lodge. When it was first being constructed, he helped freight in all the boats, motors, furniture, and building supplies.

Naturally out of all Pan's activities came stories of his practical jokes, played on friends and strangers alike. Freighting is no exception; however the tale we relate here is about someone making Pan the brunt of the prank, a thing that happened rarely. It was told to us by several different people, each one adding on to it, so we believe we have the complete facts.

Pan had come into Anahim Lake, by team and sleigh, for supplies. As usual, he stayed on for a few days, bedding down at Thomas Squinas, an Indian friend's house, spending the time gossiping and bending elbows.

Ready to return to the Home Ranch, Pan pulled up to Christensen's store to load. Ed Collett, who worked for Andy, was hobbling around on crutches. The situation was a natural for Pan and his idea of humor; he badgered and teased Ed about breaking his leg, "probably in jumping out a bedroom window in the middle of the night," or a few other figments of his vivid imagination. Ed rolled with the punch lines and returned Pan's grin for grin.

Finally, as all good things must come to an end, Pan had his sleigh loaded, the team ready, and was prepared to set out around the mountain for home. Several of his cronies had come to the store that morning, so went out on the porch to wave goodbye. Pan failed to tumble that they had been tipped off to be sure and be watching this particular departure.

He got up on the seat, tucked his big coat in around his bum, grabbed the reins, yelled, "So long!" slapped the lines on the horses' rumps, and disappeared in a cloud of powdery snow. But the sleigh stayed put. It was Pan on his stomach, still clutching the reins, being towed behind horses doing a full run, while yelling, "Whoa you sonsa bitches!" at the top of his lungs. The team ran in a circle stopping back near the sleigh, where a delighted audience picked Pan from the snow, mad but not hurt.

Using the excuse that he had to take a leak, Ed had hobbled out to Pan's rig and pulled the pin from the double tree, replacing it with a small stick. When the four horse team leaned into the harness, the only thing that moved was Pan, flying off the seat into the snow when the stick broke. Knowing, that with no load behind them plus being spooked by the yelling, Pan didn't dare let loose of the lines, or the horses might run all the way to Holtes' place so all Pan could do was hang on.

His buddies had doubled over in laughter, reveling in the fact they had been able to put the shoe on the other foot this time. Pan had taken the bait and not even suspected the trick. He didn't think it was all that great of a joke either.

"Ranch life in the Blackwater was a matter of survival-
-cattle first, people second."

——George Aitken

THE SECOND FAMILY

Pan met Adelia ("Shorty") at a dance in Bella Coola, when he was in town with a pack train picking up supplies. Later he learned that she worked in the hotel he stayed at and managed to chat with her in the halls on occasion. At that particular time every romantic young lady's thoughts turned to the man in the dirty shirt, sweat stained Stetson, cowboy boots, and chaps. Cowboys were the rage, and Pan rode high on the tide, taking care never to get his shirt too clean, nor take off his chaps. One thing he continued to do religiously, however, was to get his hair cut.

So Shorty saw, swooned, and set her sights on this hawk nosed Yank with the engaging smile and good sense of humour. The cowboy complex reigned supreme in her mind.

Chaps were the obvious sign of a low paying job in those days and Shorty's parents, Miles and Johana Brewester, took a dim view of her facination for Pan. Many a family swore they would not "have a pair of chaps in their family." Ranch Romance magazines saw it differently as did their readers, and Shorty was an avid fan. Marrying a cowboy was her fantasy.

Alfred Bryant knew Shorty and her family and when he needed help with the cooking, during haying season at the Tallywacker Ranch, he invited her to come up to help out. This she did. Moccasin telegraph* or whatever, one way or another, Pan got word of her presence at Alfred's and was soon astride a horse headed that way. It didn't take more than about two trips around the mountain, for Pan to convince Shorty that she should come on out to the Home Ranch to cook, after she finished working for Alfred. She agreed and Pan set a date to pick her up.

---

* The moccasin telegraph, that unexplainable phenomenon of the Chilcotin and Blackwater country, has baffled white men since they first came to that country. No wires, no telegraph key yet news spread like wildfire through the country, without any visible personal contact. A tidbit of gossip could outrace the fastest rider, as if the natives were masters of ESP.

He arrived the day before the assigned date and the Bryant cabin rocked that night, as the end of haying season was heralded with a party. The next morning, bright (the day, most certainly not Pan) and early, they departed on the long ride to the Home Ranch. Arriving late in the evening, Pan led a stiff and sore Shorty (all 4', 11" and 95 pounds - ready to collapse) into the unfinished, new house and pointing to a pile of straw in the corner, told her, "There's your bed." He then went into the next room to his own rough cut lumber bed, with a straw mattress, and proceeded to turn in. If he thought the straw in the corner might prompt Shorty into entering into a more compromising arrangement, he got fooled.

However, in about three months, around Christmas time, they were on their way into Quesnel, to get hitched. Word got to them that their friends in the Anahim Lake area were planning a party for them and they returned that way. There has been some 'dos', some 'bashes', some 'busts', and just plain parties, but no one has ever come up with an adjective to describe the celebration for Pan and Shorty, held at the Clesspocket Ranch. It is still a topic of conversation around campfires in the Chilcotin and Blackwater country. Every man, woman, child, Indian and his dog showed up for it.

On their return to the Home Ranch, Pan tied into finishing the house inside and Shorty got her first insight of Pan's thrifty nature when she unfolded some curtains, she had bought for the house, and began to put them up. First Pan griped about the cost and then when they were up he griped about the loss of light in the house. "Jesus Christ, that's what we hauled them windows in here for was to get some light in the house and here you go shutting it out with your fancy dodads," Pan chided her.

Shorty was a hard worker and a good housekeeper and Pan soon found out she was worth making some concessions for, like ultimately installing locks on the doors. This after much grumbling. "Who the hell needs locks out here? Ain't no grizzly I ever heard of could turn a door knob." But locked doors were a fettish with Shorty.

Their life together had its good moments and its bad. At first they were very much in love, but Pan's worries about the operation and finances of the F.C.C. sometimes showed in his mood. He wasn't always the understanding husband.

In the winter, Pan did most of his freighting, which usually left Shorty alone at the ranch to feed the hired hands. On one occasion, when Pan was away, and while the crew was out feeding the stock Ila Holte, who had become fast friends with Shorty, was visiting, they ran out of wood. With the pile completely depleted, Ila got a bit excited, as any young girl might be expected to. "We'll freeze. It's 40 degrees below, outside!"

"No we won't. I know where there's some wood," Shorty replied and promptly took an axe to the partition between the kitchen and dining room. Pan returned to find the whole west end of the house one big room. We won't quote his remarks here, but the partition was never replaced.

When Shorty was six months along with their first child, Pan figured she would be better off with her parents in Bella Coola, so he saddled up two horses and threw a pack saddle on the third one for her personal gear. With Gin, the ranch pooch, running alongside, they set out on the long 150 mile (approximate) trek to Bella Coola.

On the trail at night, Gin slept with Shorty, providing some warmth for her in the cold temperatures. She would have liked to have kept him in Bella Coola with her, but Gin was Pan's squirrel and cow dog and was needed back at the ranch, as hunting squirrels brought in part of the family income above what Pan was supposed to get as foreman for the cattle company. Originally, Pan had traded a bottle of gin for the dog and then sat on a log and helped the Indian empty the bottle. "Figure the dog only cost me half a bottle, that way," Pan told Rich Boland one time.

After the baby, a girl they named Gayle, was born Pan again made the trip to Bella Coola with the horses to pick up Shorty and the child. Shorty had rigged up an Indian basket with cheese cloth over the top to protect the baby from flies and mosquitoes and Pan fixed some rigging so that it would be easy for her to manage the basket on the long ride.

The following summer, Shorty had a tooth that was giving her fits, so she got word to the Holte Ranch that she needed some help. Hattie and her daughters, Ila and Alyce, rode over with their gear to baby sit Gayle and do the cooking at the ranch. When they arrived, it was decided that Ila would ride along with Shorty to Vanderhoof. Her

"SHORTY" (Adelia) and Pan, with daughter Gayle, at the Home Ranch.

mother and sister would stay at the ranch.

Pan took note of the fact that among the things Shorty had laid out to load on the packhorse was a fair amount of food. "You don't need to lug all that grub along. Just take your 30-30 and you two can live off the fat of the land. Plenty of rabbits and spruce hens out now," he told her. Whether he was kidding or not, Shorty ended the discussion by making a suggestion as to where Pan could put the spruce hens and rabbits.

During the period of time, when Ila and Shorty were gone, a drifter cowboy came riding through, looking for work and Pan took him on. It wasn't long before this fellow really took a shine to Alyce and began to pester her. He touched and pinched her leg whenever he had the chance and when it got past the point of 'funnin,' Alyce confronted him about it, in front of her mother and Pan. Needless to say, Hattie hit the roof and Pan, quick to assess the situation, knew it was better to lose a hand than a cook and baby sitter, so he fired the man on the spot. "Can't have no shenanigans like that going on around here. You hit the trail, now, fast!" Pan bellowed, more for Hattie's sake than to vent his own feelings.

Pan figured he was losing a hand, but no use letting the chance for a little fun pass by, so just as the rider went through the first gate Pan started yelling. "No! Don't shoot Mrs. Holte! You might kill him!" And with that announcement, whipped out his six-shooter and fired a couple shots in the air while still yelling, "No! No! Don't shoot, don't shoot!"

The cowboy never realized he'd been had by the master prankster and went racing down the trail quite sure he was about to be shot off his horse by Hattie Holte.

"Must have ridden clear out of the country," Alyce told us. "He's never been seen since."

The next winter, Christmas came late to the ranch. It wasn't until mid-January that Pan got back from a freight run with the mail and they spent several pleasant evenings going through the cards, reading, re-reading and relishing every word. Among the packages were gifts for Gayle, her only Christmas present to that time being a crib, handcrafted by George Aitken, the young hired hand.

Shorty remembers the next Christmas for another reason. Pan was a careful drinker yet he appeared to out drink everyone else. He stretched his drinks, and though never having an empty hand or glass, he didn't seem to get staggering drunk. But on this Christmas Day, the freshly acquired liquor, that came in on the freight sleigh, got to Pan. Perhaps, it was the fact that he hadn't had a drink for quite a spell, the heat of the room, or the altitude, but whatever, Pan was inebriated and put on his own version of a wild west show right in the house. He ended up by shooting his 44 at various and sundry objects in the house, including the tree ornaments, while Shorty pleaded with him to, "Put the gun away before you kill someone, or hurt yourself." But bullets continued to fly and if you are ever in the old ranch house, you can still see the holes in some of the logs. Pan made no points with Shorty that day.

Again Shorty became pregnant and this time Pan had her farmed out at the Bryants, where Jane Bryant, (RN), the 'Florence Nightingale of the Chilcotin,' could look after her. One day, Shorty borrowed a team and sleigh to go into Anahim Lake to the store. On the way back, the team spooked and ran away with her. When a runner hit a hummock in the meadow the team was running through, Shorty was pitched out on the ground and had the wind knocked out of her. The team ended up in the ranch yard and the Bryants immediately backtracked them and found Shorty.

Alfred was told of the accident and asked to get Pan. He saddled up and rode for the Home Ranch, carrying a written message from Jane. It took him a day and a half of hard riding to get there, but somehow Pan misinterpreted the note and didn't hit the trail until the next morning, leaving Alfred to do his chores. New snow slowed him down and by the time he got to the Bryants, two days later, Shorty had aborted.

Another time, Shorty began having pains in her side, and Pan, suspecting that it might be an attack of appendicitis, sent George to the Holtes to phone for a float plane to come in and get her. George made a record ride and the weather co-operated. Soon Shorty and baby Gayle were winging their way into Quesnel. When George got back, he told Pan, "She's gonna have company. Ila Holte is in the hospital too, with appendicitis."

"Jesus Christ. Those two been getting so close as friends, they gotta do everything together," Pan remarked.

Alex Fraser, Pan's friend in Quesnel, and his wife Gertrude, met the plane. Gertrude took Gayle home to care for, after depositing Shorty in the hospital. It was appendicitis and she was operated on immediately, sharing a room with Ila Holte. Both girls then stayed with the Frasers for a couple of weeks while they recuperated.

Pan's thrifty nature came to the fore again and instead of sending a plane for Shorty and Gayle, he came to town with the team and wagon to pick them up. A hundred and fifty mile ride, back to the ranch, in the wagon with a small child, just to save the price of a plane ride, didn't make any points with Shorty either.

Shorty was a hard worker and once back on her feet, she continued with her chores. She cooked for the ranch hands, washed clothes in a tub using a hand wash board, packed water from the creek in tin pails, chopped wood for the kitchen range, worked to feed the haying crews at the outlying meadows, fished for food for the table, shot moose, and in general made every effort to be a good rancher's wife. To help keep their heads above water, she baked 27 loaves of bread in one day to pay the haying crew, in lieu of cash. But somehow the romance in their relationship ebbed until one day they agreed to disagree for good. It came after an argument over a pair of chaps, Rich Hobson's wife Gloria, had given Shorty.

By this time, Shorty was pregnant again and Pan knew when she rode out of the yard, for the last time, that he might never see her again. First she went to Bella Coola, then to the lower mainland and finally to Victoria. The second child, Elaine, was born a few months after she had left. Pan managed to keep track of Shorty and the girls through friends, Gayle returning for summer holidays and to work, later.

"No one ever heard a bad word about Pan Phillips."
————Jack Maxwell

THE NEW CANADIAN CITIZEN

Pan had began to build a close friendship with Alex Fraser, a friendship that lasted the remainder of his life.

Fraser felt an equal kindred spirit toward Pan and his well-being was often on Alex's mind, so after Britain had declared war on Germany, Alex gave Pan some advice.

"You'd better get your Canadian citizenship papers soon because the U.S. is bound to get into this mess and you could very easily get a notice you've been drafted. Up here in B.C., you'll undoubtedly be exempt because of your cattle ranching, but that won't cut any ice down in the States."

It didn't take too long for those sage words of advice to sink in and Pan soon sent out word that he sure would like for Alex to go to Victoria with him to say a few words at his hearing. Also, if he could get Dave Smith, from the Quesnel hardware store, to vouch for him, too, it would be appreciated

It didn't take Alex long either, to get things set up and send word back to Pan. They were soon off to Victoria.

At his hearing, Pan drew a 'tough judge' by the name of Henry Castillio. He was fair, but he had a reputation for giving no concessions. This worried Pan somewhat, as the judge had been to Anahim Lake hunting and stories of the way his gavel dropped, had spread.

Alex was first on the witness stand and was asked why he was there. "I'm here to vouch for Floyd Phillips and am in favour of giving him his citizenship papers."

"How do you know he's not a cattle rustler from the States, come up here to get away from the sheriff?" asked the judge.

"I've known him for several years and consider him a good honest man. He has been a good customer of my father's store, John A. Frazer Company, Ltd. in Quesnel. He's met all his obligations promptly," was Alex reply. He continued on with several other reasons he thought might sway the judge's decision in Pan's favor.

Pan sat there on the hard bench getting more nervous by the minute. He was squirming and beginning to sweat like a hog being led to the boiler, all of which did not escape his honour's sharp eye.

The judge excused Alex, and Dave Smith took the stand. Basically, he reiterated Alex's words. By this time, sweat was running down Pan's face and his underarms were soaked. It was his turn now.

"Well, Mr. Phillips, I don't think I'm going yo give you your papers now, but while you're here I'll listen to you."

Pan walked to the witness stand, with sweat running off his hawk nose like tap water. He apologized for being nervous, and pointed out that his entire future was at stake. Getting control of himself a bit, he went on to tell the judge of his plans for the ranch; how cattle from it would be of great value to the country in the inevitable and trying war years ahead; dispelled any fears that he was a criminal of any type; and in general made a very good impression. Once he got to talking, his forthright honesty, apparent integrity, and enthusiasm for the country, began to crack the aloof armour of the judge. Finally, after Pan had gotten his second wind and his sweating curtailed, he was excused, with a comment that caused Pan to breathe a huge sigh of relief.

"I've changed my mind, Mr. Phillips. I will recommend you for your Canadian Citizenship and futher more, I'll give you a high enough recommendation that your papers won't get tied up on someone else's desk."

Pan had them 60 days later and the U.S. lost its chance to get a hell of a tough cowboy into uniform.

"Pan wasn't a handyman, especially around the house;
he was scared of anything with a handle on it."
——Betty Phillips

THE THIRD FAMILY

For a year and a half, after Shorty left, Pan tried to get by without a regular cook, but it was getting "plumb lonesome" around the place and the crew wasn't exactly in love with the boiled grub he kept setting out for them. So he began casting about for a replacement.

It came about that Alfred Bryant, on one of his freight trips, ran across a tall dark, good looking divorcee, working in the pulp and paper mill, at Ocean Falls. He told her about the big ranch up in the Blackwater country that needed a cook. She didn't have to give it too much thought as she told us, "Alfred mentioned that this ranch needed a cook badly, and since I always liked that country, I decided to take on the job, which I did, and later became Pan's wife"

A little more communication between the two, via Alfred, led to a date for the arrival of Betty Kushner, at Quesnel, aboard the twice a week PG&E (nicknamed the Please Go Easy) railroad.

Pan drove a team and wagon into town, arriving ahead of the train's schedule, and headed for Alex Fraser's where a few belts of O.P. rum began to take the kinks out. As it neared the arrival time, Alex accompanied Pan to the depot to meet his new cook. On the platform they encountered, McNeil, another friend, waiting for his wife to arrive on the same train. Pan took on a bit more 'relaxment' from McNeil's bottle, who was already 'corned' - it was a jolly little group that awaited the train.

The old steam engine came puffing into the depot, with it's string of antiquated passenger cars, and when Betty stepped off, Pan was speechless. She was one, plumb beautiful woman and his corpuscles did a flip flop. After a bit of celebration in town, with Pan introducing his new cook to all his friends, Betty and he sat out on the long ride to the Home Ranch. It was mid July 1943, hot and the mosquitoes were out with voracious appetites. Betty was about to learn the big difference between living on the coast and the interior.

The wagon bounced and jolted over timber and rocks and the hard board seat began to blister her bum. Soon, she ached in every joint. Pan had failed to tell her, that if she wasn't used to riding in a wagon, that she should hop off every few miles and walk out the stiffness.

By late afternoon, on the second day, Betty was beat and started dozing, That was her first mistake, for no one had told her about Pan's proneness to playing practical jokes and tricks. Pan, noting her nodding head, just couldn't resist the opporunity to have some fun. As they went through the woods he reached out grabbed a branch, held it for a second as they moved forward, then ducked and let it loose. The branch flew back and hit Betty in the chin. She woke up startled and nearly fell off the seat. When she figured out what had happened, and why, Pan immediately became acutely aware that Betty had acquired a fair vocabulary while working in the mill.

Betty loved new experiences. This was one of the factors in her teaming up with Pan and she soon found that they came by the gross at the ranch. She followed Shorty's footsteps in cooking for Pan and the hands; washed their clothes in a big tub using a scrub board; carried two pails of water at the same time from the creek by using a yoke over her shoulders; sawed and chopped wood for the kitchen range; canned meat and vegetables; helped with the haying; and later took over all the garden work. In essence, she worked from daylight until dark, seven days a week. Pan wasn't religious and Sunday was just another day at the ranch, The new experiences were not exactly what she had bargained for, but soon it became a way of life for her.

However, all was not smooth sailing over the years. It seemed that Pan and Betty dearly loved to make up, but in order to do that, first they had to have a fight, so their joys in making up were many. Their fights became legend, but love seemed to win over as they always patched things up.

When Betty first came to the Home Ranch, she had the meals on the table right on time and was considerably upset when the men would come straggling in a half hour or hour late to eat. By then, her carefully prepared meal would be overcooked, dried out, and the meat would have the resiliency of a leather boot. While cleaning house one day, she discovered a whistle, left there by someone unknown. This led to formulation of a plan for salvaging her meals. In no uncertain terms, she announced, later, to Pan and the hands, "When I blow my whistle, I want you all to drop whatever you're doing and come in to eat instantly! Is that understood?"

"You might jist as well shove that whistle up yer ass. How the hell we gonna hear it if we're out in the pasture someplace." Pan snorted. Round one in favour of Pan Phillips.

Pan expected Betty to cut all the wood for the house, which she did. Either he or one of the hands would haul in the logs and from there on it was Betty's department. He had other ranch chores more important to do for the men and himself he figured. As a result, Betty bucked the logs with a Swede saw, split the blocks, and packed it in to the woodbox. At first, she treated it as a joke, telling the hands to "Go get the cook some wood." They all just ignored her, so she would do it.

Then she would tease Pan about hating physical work, trying to shame him into getting some wood for her. But those efforts failed, too. The hints went on for considerable time, Betty still carrying on with the heavy chore. Then they hauled in a load of wet logs, from near the river, that bound up the saw everytime, halfway through the cut. Betty went on strike.

The next time Pan and the crew showed up for the noon meal, Betty was sitting in the front room reading.

"What the hell you doin' woman? Where's dinner?"

"Peers the wood box is empty and I can't saw that crap you hauled in, so no wood - no dinner, and that goes from now on."

The crew ate cold sandwiches. After dinner, Pan went out to try to saw the wood. He tried a few cuts, then gave up and sent George out for a load of dry timber. The next day, he left for a load of supplies and when he returned, the boys helped him unload a buzz saw that was adaptable to the 'power take off' on the tractor. From that time on, Betty had the logs bucked up for her, but she still had to do most of the splitting. Round two in favour of Betty Phillips.

And so it went. Flying objects (not UFOs) were not a rarity around the ranch. Betty had a good right arm and a temper to match. Pan became adept at ducking. If Betty erupted, Pan would wisely retreat to the corral, saddle up and ride out to check anything-the cattle, the fences, the horses - coming back only after he thought she was cooled off some.

Most of these episodes, Pan brought on himself for he would tease and taunt Betty until she came to the end of her rope and explode. Then they would shout and hollar to get it out of their systems. Half the time Pan would leave the house chuckling. Neither could claim a win in those rounds.

Betty had learned to cook many things she had never been exposed to before, like moose meat which was a daily fare, spruce hens and ducks ran a close second. Fish she was more used to after living on the coast, and were plentiful in the creek, although it took time to catch them. During the fall round-up and branding season, after Betty arrived, Pan told her he expected "A big mountain oyster feed."

"I know what oysters are, but what's a mountain oyster?"

"Nuts, to you," was Pan's short answer.

She thought he was kidding, but when she asked one of the crew, he replied, "Sure ain't."

Pan assured her that they were the most expensive thing on the menu at the Waldorf Astoria in New York, so she grudgingly agreed to cook up a batch. When the first pail full was brought to the house for her to clean and cook, she couldn't believe what she was about to do. Talk about a new experience - that was it.

But after watching Pan and the help wade through a whole platter full of the fried delicacies, she decided to give them a try herself. "Those dammed things are really scrumptous," she declared.

When Pan had to be away freighting or trapping, Betty was left alone at the ranch, as in winter they sometimes did not have help. Once when he was gone, the mercuty dropped to the bottom of the bulb, reading 75 degrees below zero (f). Kluskus Tommy, who had become a good friend and didn't live too far, rode over every few days to check on her and their tiny son Kenneth. Betty made her appreciation to the native's friendship evident, realizing that behind the visits was Pan's ongoing congenial relationship with all the Indians in which he made them equal.

One time after Betty was no longer just 'the hired cook,' all kind thoughts about the Indians fled her mind, however, It was a spring day and several native families were camped nearby. She hadn't seen Pan for hours; neither had she seen George and the wood shed was almost empty, Betty suspected that Pan and George might be visiting. Time went on and she became more vexed by the minute.

Glancing out the window, she spied them, and the green eyed monster, known as jealously, claimed her, mind and body. Pan was strolling up towards the house with his arm around one very well endowed young Indian girl, and George was following, his arm around another young girl. Pan was chattering away, grinning like he was in horse heaven, and George looked like a cat that had got into the cream. Betty became infuriated. As they were coming up the walk, the kitchen door flew open and Betty met them with a big pan full of scalding hot, boiling potatoes she'd had on the stove. Yelling an obscenity at Pan, she threw the hot water, potatoes, and pan at them all. They ducked and scattered like a covey of quail someone had taken a shot at.

"Jesus Christ, Jesus Christ!" Pan yelled as he scampered off in one direction, George in the other, and the two Indian girls in another.

Later Pan told Betty, "Damn, you shouldna done that Betty. You could've burned one of us, bad. We was jist bringing them over fer coffee to show how friendly we are here at the ranch. I wouldn't touch one of those gals nohow."

"Yeah, I'll bet."

The battle was over. The monster released Betty and things went on as normal around the place, except George gave Betty a wide berth for a while afterwards.

Pan was sitting in his favourite chair, by the heater, one day, when Betty came into the kitchen with the usual two pails of water. She began complaining to him about having to carry water and how heavy it was. Pan gave her remarks a minute to sink in, then replied, "Christ, woman, don't be a damned fool. Only fill the pails half full and make two trips." He went back to cutting shavings for the next morning's fire. Betty started for him, a pail of water in her hand, but Pan moved faster and barricaded himself in the bedroom for a spell, just missing a total drenching.

It seemed to Betty that nearly everyone in the Blackwater had some kind of small herd of their own, cattle or horses or both. Soon she realized that cattle was the only sign of wealth and accomplishment to Indians and whites alike.

"How you going to pay me for the extra work I put in haying this year?" she asked Pan one morning. "The rest of my work may come under the usual 'womans work' but slaving away out there in the field in the hot sun and mosquitoes, is something else."

"Guess you're right. How about I give you a calf for yer wages?"

From this meager start Betty gained additional cattle each year, which multiplied and eventually, she was the owner of a small herd, under her own brand, all of which seemed to please Pan.

Upon returning from a freight trip one day, Pan pulled the wagon up in front of the house, and called Betty. She rushed out of the house in time to see him unloading a gas powered washing machine. With vivid memories of the countless back breaking hours over a washboard, Pan suddenly became the epitome of her greatest hero. She showered him with thanks, love and affection. Pan lapped it all up - until the day she learned he had sold one of her cows to buy the washer. Pan grabbed some moose jerky, his bedroll, and lit out for the far range to check cattle for a few days. Betty knew without asking why he had not used his own money. "Whatever he could get his hands on, he hoarded, thinking about the 'rainy days' ahead," she declared.

The washing machine worked beautifully. It gave Betty more hours for her other chores, so in her heart she forgave him, but the thought of getting even lingered.

Later the chance was given to her by little Ken, who had been nicknamed "Willie" by Pan because, as he told Betty, "Kenneth's just too damn sissyfied a name for him. He looks like a Willie to me." And it stayed Willie until he left the ranch to make his own way. Willie was great for stuffing his overall pockets with rocks, nuts, bolts, nails, and about anything else he could find laying about. Betty usually carefully checked his clothes over before dropping them in the washer, but one day, she missed a bolt which then worked it's way down under the agitiator. By the time the washing was done, to her dismay, she found the tub leaking. The bolt had worn a hole through the metal.

She called it to Pan's attention and he shrugged it off. "Hold yer finger under the hole, like the little Dutch kid," jockingly ignoring the problem.

However, the next time Pan took out his good Stetson to go into town, you could hear him bellowing clear across the meadow. A sizeable chunk of the brim was missing, that being the only thing Betty could find to use as a gasket to repair the leaky tub. It held perfectly and never again leaked, but Pan was far from appreciative of Betty's ingenuity.

In 1945, three weeks before Diana was born, Pan sent Betty into Quensel, while she could still ride a horse. When the tiny infant entered the world, she almost had a short stay, as she had excessive mucous in her lungs. Betty sent a radio message to Pan, via the Prince George network. (In 1957, the Quesnel, Williams Lake, and 100 Mile House radio network aired their first message hour and reception at the Home Ranch was much better.) The message let Pan know when she would be ready to return.

Pan couldn't see how he could take the time away from the ranch duties, so he sent George in with the Bennett buggy to retrieve Betty and the new little one. Pan had rigged up a basket, of sorts for Diana but on the way in, George lost it off the wagon, so Diana made her first trip through the Blackwater, in a Pacific Milk carton atop the supplies.

Eleven years later, Rob was born and it was a repeat performance, except Betty had begun to have trouble with arthritis and Pan had sent her into town four months before the baby was due. She lost 48 pounds in six weeks and after chiropractic treatments, was able to have a normal birth. Pan was kept advised of the situation by her radio messages, which were listened to, a topic of conversation by all those in the area that had access to a battery powered radio.

When Betty finally arrived back home, Pan again disagreed with her on the name and snorted, "Robert Eugene! Jesus Christ!" He stomped out in the yard for a smoke. Eugene was his middle name and he hated it worse than Floyd, so his newest son became Robbie.

THE FAMILY FACES CHANGED as the years passed. This shows Pan and Betty, and children Diana and "Willie" (Ken), at the Home Ranch.

Betty tutoured the kids at home when they were school age, using the government supplied correspondence courses. Pan shied away from helping them with the lessons, stating that he wasn't up on "all that new fangled stuff." Eventually, it proved to be too much extra work for her and Pan arranged to have the kids boarded out at friend's homes or sent to boarding school.

Betty was fond of flowers and plants. Whenever she was in town she tried to get starts and had geraniums, ivy and shamrock plants growing in the house, making a real home out of the mess she had walked into after Pan's batching. Pan, on the other hand, would have been content with bare walls. He didn't object to her doilies and feminine nickknacks about the house, yet he never bought her any additional ones.

Sometime, after Rob's birth, Betty went back into Quesnel for a check up as she wasn't feeling well. The doctor told her she had a tumor. She decided to return home, though, by then accepting the 150 mile ride, either by wagon or horseback, as a city woman might an auto ride to the next town. Once there, she grew progressively worse and Pan arranged for her to go to Vancouver, to have the tumor removed. It turned out to be a nine and half pound growth, benign. But her health troubles escalated, and further trips for arthritis treatments, in Vancouver, on her hands and hips were necessary. Pan, the kids and crew made do for themselves while she was away.

"Pan Phillips has a great place over those mountains.
Well hid, too!"

—Andy Christensen

THE HOME RANCH

The Home Ranch house was of log construction, with a sod roof. It had six rooms at first, but was later reduced to four rooms after Shorty used one kitchen partition for firewood and Betty knocked out a bedroom wall to make two rooms into one large master bedroom.

The back door (or side door) opened dierctly into the kitchen. Straight through was the eating area. The big old kitchen range and woodbox, stood on the right. Later, cupboards, constructed and hauled in by Rex Bartlett, as a gift to Betty, replaced the long rough wooden shelves on the left. On another of his fifteen visits, he brought, then installed a sink, which drained into a drywell outside.

Three bedrooms joined the kitchen on the south side of the building and the balance of the house facing the north side, was one big living room with a heater by the north wall. Later, a fireplace was built where the heater sat, after Bob Anthony bought the ranch.

The floors were of rough planking, until in the 1960s, when Pan hauled in plywood, which was laid down and varnished. Also, somewhere along the years, the log walls were covered with plywood inside and Betty ordered in flowered wall paper from the mail order catalogue.

The happy laughter of children rang through the house over the years. Gayle lived there until her mother, Shorty, left with her when she was four; Willie was raised in the house until he was old enough to leave home, at 17, to work elsewhere; Diana and Rob grew up and lived there until the ranch was sold, with the odd sabatical from ranch life, while attending boarding school or working out, in the winter.

Elaine first came to the ranch when Gayle and she visited in the summers, bringing the grandchildren.

Pan loved to tease the kids and would keep at it until he got them to scrapping then he'd come "Hee hee"-ing into the house to tell Betty, "Your kid and my kids are fighting with our kids."

A root cellar kept their vegetables reasonably cool and

a screened in meat house, by the creek, kept insects away from the meat. When it began to get really hot, Betty canned the meat to save it.

As the children grew older, Willie moved into the bunkhouse with the men and Diana created her own private boudoir in the loft over the ice house.

Pan had constructed the ice house from unpeeled logs and later as the bark came off, it would leave holes between the logs, letting the sawdust to spill out. Diana spent many of her young hours keeping the walls well chinked.

The log cabin, Tom and Andy Holte built in 1935, that later became the bunkhouse, had a puncheon floor, a rough lumber table, a bench and four single, jackpine pole bunks with hay mattresses. It was approximately 10'x14' and well placed under a stand of trees facing the creek. It has (1985) the original windows, one a 2'x4', none of which opened. As a result, the occupants had to leave the door open to get air, which in turn let in the mosquitoes and bugs. The hands had no complaints about cleanliness, as Betty 'dunged it out' once a week "whether it needed it or not."

The outhouse provided several different services; it not only was a place to relieve oneself, but it provided sort of a sanctuary. One could review the articles offered for sale in the previous years Simpson Sears catalogue; Pan could spend a few minutes while Betty cooled off from a spat; the kids could fritter away time until someone else brought in the 'jingle horse',* and best of all, through the open door, there was the best view of the northern lights on the ranch.

The store Pan built to serve the area and make a few extra dollars, was a 12'x 16' log building. Beans, rice and other dried foodstuffs were stored in barrels. Flour and sugar came by the sacks. The door was in the narrow end, and as you walked in, the counter was on the right, with shelves behind. Merchandise, such as traps and rope, hung by nails on the opposite wall and far end. There was a drawer for money under the counter. Furs were gladly accepted in lieu of legal tender and cattle were sometimes traded for goods. No food left the store for the cook in the kitchen; that was kept in a seperate larder.

---

* A belled horse kept close enough to the ranch house to be caught easily, saddled and ridden out to catch whatever other horses they needed.

Patrons of the Home Ranch store were mostly Indian neighbours, with an occasional drifter stopping by for a plug of tobacco, or trail grub. Many of the natives would travel up to thirty or more miles from Kluskus, Paley's store there having closed some years before. They usually camped overnight on the creekbank behind the store. If it was cold, and there was an empty bunk in the bunkhouse, Pan would offer to let them stay there.

Pan set the prices on all items, however sometimes he let the dollar signs in his eyeballs get the best of him and put on too high a price. Once in a while this made a customer unhappy when he found the same item later in town at a fraction of Pan's price. Peter Alexis, Pan's closest native friend, was one of the store's regular customers over the years. He never beefed about the prices, knowing what most drifters failed to consider and that was the amount of work and time required to freight in the supplies.

Even Pan's store customers didn't escape his pranks. Once when he turned in a list that ordered shoelaces among a hundred other items, Alf Legler had trouble deciphering some of his hieroglyphics and gave him about twice as many as he wanted. They came in boxes with the price clearly printed on each package of laces; ten cents being the retail price.

Discovering he had twice as many as he needed to stock his shelves, Pan decided what his store needed was a sale, so he put up a sign and passed the word to all the natives he met, "Big sale," two packages for 25¢. No Indian customer left the store without getting in on Pan's big deal. Everytime he made a shoelace sale he "Hee-hee"-ed it up.

"What's gonna happen when those Indians find out you've played a trick on them?" Willie asked his Dad.

"Damnfino. We'll wait and see."

Not too many moons passed before the natives figured out what was going on, but instead of getting upset, they seemed to think it was a good joke. "Pan Phillips, he fool us." They had been flim flammed, but seemed to enjoy it. It goes without saying that that prank kept the moccasin telegraph going for awhile.

During a particulary heavy snowfall one winter, the weight collapsed the roof on the store and Pan had to dig out his merchandise from under a ton of sod and broken poles. He used the old logs for firewood and rebuilt the roof, amid considerable grumbling.

The store did quite well during the Frontier Cattle Co. days, but afterwards business seemed to fall off, undoubtedly due to word being spread about the demise of the company, the lack of drifters and no large crew, due to the war. However, Pan continued to operate it for several more years.

"Pan, he treated my people good. He was my very good
friend since he come to the Blackwater."
—Peter Alexis

DUSTING OFF THE WELCOME MAT

Visitors at the Home Ranch were probably more
welcome than anywhere else in the world and the natives
were no exception. It was a lonely life and visits were
cherished.

In the fall and winter months, when most whites
traveled little, the natives were usually the only outsiders
the Phillips family and crew had for company. Every week
or so, Pan could count on either the Alexis family, the
Cassams, the Squinas family, or the Baptistes to come by.
Some weren't long on conversation, but just their presence
in the house broke the feeling of total isolation. The
Indians were experienced winter travelers and time hung
heavy on their hands, so they needed an excuse to go
visiting.

A visit from anyone, winter or summer, was all that
Pan needed to drop whatever he was doing and in his
inimitable style, entertain the guests. Perhaps his sister,
Hazel Seeds, tells it best.

"I made three visits to beautiful British Columbia, but
the trip I will never forget was the summer of 1949. I was
eighteen and Mother, two brothers and I drove to Anahim
Lake and rode by horseback to the Home Ranch. In 1949,
Diana and Willie (Ken) were about four and five years old
and the Home Ranch was a working ranch. We hunted,
fished, swam in the river, branded cattle, killed a moose-
cleaned it and enjoyed eating it, put up hay, mended fences
and enjoyed a snow storm in the mountains. Betty and Pan
were younger and in love and made our visit marvelous."

"During the trip from Anahim Lake to the Home
Ranch by horse back, over the mountains, Pan was on
cloud nine showing us his beautiful British Columbia and
we discovered just how great an out-doors-man he was."

Another sister, Betty Bradshaw wrote, "My husband
and I and two of our children were fortunate enough to
make two trips to the Home Ranch. These trips will always

be remembered. Pan always took care of the one in need. While I was visiting, the sole came off my boot while we were at the far end of a lake area, so instead of me having to walk back, he took me as far as he could in a boat."

"Also, he realized I was a poor rider so the horse he picked for me to ride was as gentle as a kitten and knew just how to get an inexperienced rider up the mountain and down again."

Wanderers were treated as well, though, and once three young men stumbled into the ranch footsore, needing a good meal and looking for work. Hungry for fresh conversation, Pan felt sorry for them. He gave them a job loading gravel from the creek onto a wagon, the gravel to be used for damming irrigation ditches.

Those young fellows were of the Bahai faith, not too ambitious, and spent considerable time leaning on their shovels discussing worldly religious problems. Pan said little, but listened in on their conversation with interest. One of their talks led to an argument, a loud yelling match. Pan, in the corral, heard the rucus and ran out to the creek to see what was going on. The lads ignored his attempts at peacemaking until he yelled, "God damn it! Make love - not war!" They didn't last long at the ranch.

Pan, sitting in his rocker late one afternoon, had already lit the gas lamp and hung it on the rafter overhead, when a plane was heard in the vicinity of the ranch.

"Hey, Pan, I think someone's going to land on the lake," George Aitken called across the room.

In his excitement at the prospect of a visitor, Pan jumped up. His head hit the lamp and it crashed to the floor, fuel spilling. Quick as a flash, to prevent a fire, Pan grabbed the lamp and threw it out the front room window, smashing the glass to bits. The plane flew on by - false alarm for the lonely people plus Pan had to contemplate the loss of the window glass and the lamp. Betty wisely held her tongue.

One winter day, Floyd Vaughan and John Blackwell, neighbours from Moose Lake Lodge, came roaring out of the timber on snowmobiles from the north side of the big meadow. They circled around past the hay stacks, then continued on, as if they intended to take the short cut to the Pan trail thus bypassing the ranch house. Pan heard the noise, jumped to his feet and looked out to see them heading for the trees. Excitedly, he ran out into the bitter cold, sans hat and coat, yelling at the top of his lungs and waving frantically, because he thought the men and machines were going to pass right on by.

Floyd and John kept on as though they didn't see him, all the time grinning from ear to ear, but they relented at the last minute and turned their snowmobiles back towards Pan, who by then was freezing.

"Judging from all the whooping and hollaring, must be kinda lonesome around here." Floyd chortled, after the engines were shut down.

Back inside, shivering by the kitchen stove, it finally dawned on Pan that they had come purposely to visit, but decided first to have some fun at his expense. He had been bamboozled by a couple of friends and they had the last laugh. There was no "Hee hee"-ing from Pan that day.

"You've got to like ranching, as Pan did, to be in it, it's a
pretty rough game."

——Art Lavington

A MAJOR SET BACK

Ranch life, at best, was hard and cruel. For a man, like
Pan riding unbroken horses; driving skittish teams
hundreds of miles in all sorts of weather conditions;
crossing swollen, swift rivers; riding 'hell bent for leather'
through the jackpines chasing an errant steer; falling trees;
facing grizzly bears and angry moose; and a hundred and
one other dangerous activities, a serious accident was
inevitable.

'Trooper', a newly broken thoroughbred horse, was the
cause of Pan's near fatal accident, in 1948.

It was 20 degrees below zero (F), the ground had a two
foot snow cover. Pan was working a trap line with Alan
'Shag' Thompson, a young ranch hand, to augment the
ranch income. One morning as they prepared to leave,
Betty had tried to talk Pan into taking another horse, a well
broken one, for his trip out that day, but he couldn't see it
her way.

"Gotta work this horse. If we let him stand around all
winter, he won't be worth a damn come this spring when
we'll really need him."

Shag, too, was breaking in a young horse, "Silver', one
that he had bought from Pan.

It had been a hard day of fighting the snow and cold for
both the men and horses, and by late afternoon they were
anxious to get home, picking up traps along the way that
were to be reset in a different area the next day.

Pan had most of the traps tied to his saddle, and after
picking up the last one, he had to swing his leg high, to clear
them, when he mounted his horse. In this position, he was
off balance - that was when Trooper decided it was time to
try to get the man and the clanking traps off his back, by
bucking with all the energy he had left.

On a particular high, violent jump, one of the traps
flopped up into the seat as Pan came down with a thud.
Before he could control the horse or get off its back, he was

thrown high and again landed hard on the metal trap. Pan hollared in pain, then threw himself to one side as he automatically flipped his boots free of the stirrups. He fell into the snow, unconcious.

Shag was by his side in moments, applying snow to Pan's face, trying to bring him around, all the while thinking he only had the wind knocked out of him.

"Go fetch my horse," were Pan's first words on awakening. "Let me rest while yer gone. I'll be okay."

It took Shag 20 minutes to catch Trooper and lead him back to where Pan was lying. "Shag, I can't move my legs. Feel like I'm bleeding inside. Don't think I'm goin' to make it." Pan shut his eyes, groaning from the severe pain in his groin and hips.

Shag instantly turned for his horse and was already on his way as Pan muttered, "Go for help."

At the ranch corral, Shag's brother Jack, "Happy," also part of the crew, was just unhitching a team from the hay rack when he rode into the yard. "Quick, hook the team up to the empty freight sleigh and throw in some hay while I get some blankets from the bunk house - -Pan's been hurt. It's bad."

Another 20 minutes lost. All told, though, it was less than a half hour before they were beside Pan again: Happy had had the team worked into a lather before they left the big ranch meadow. But it was over an hour since the accident and by that time, the bitter cold had numbed the pain for Pan, enough so he was able to withstand their lifting him into the hay covered sleigh bed.

Betty was not aware of the accident until the team and sleigh raced up to the ranch house door. Before she could open it, Happy ran inside and excitedly told her what had happened, then asked what they could use for a stretcher. Keeping a cool head, Betty grabbed a folding cot out of the bedroom and followed Happy outside.

Pan lay still, his face ashen from the pain and cold. He couldn't speak, only moan. Betty diagnosed his condition instantly and accurately, he was suffering from hypothermia and shock.

While lifting him carefully from the sleigh onto the cot, Shag related what Pan had said about his thinking that he was bleeding internally. Betty's fear increased, the only thing she had on hand to warm him inside quickly, was brandy and she feared that might cause the bleeding to increase.

They set the cot gently by the kitchen range and opened the oven door. Pan again lapsed into unconsiousness. Extra blankets were thrown over him, but his body heat had been sapped while he lay in the snow. Betty made her decision, she would use the brandy.

Pan had clenched his jaw so hard it was almost impossible to get his mouth open, but Shag and Happy used a spoon to pry it apart slightly, then Betty managed to get a half cup of brandy into his system by patiently using an eye dropper. A few minutes later, Pan began to shake. Betty, Shag and Happy set about massaging his arms and legs to get his blood circulating and soon he was lying quiet and warm, able to talk.

Betty wanted to immediately send Shag to Anahim Lake to phone for a plane, but for some reason, Pan wouldn't hear of it. Either he thought he wasn't going to make it, or held back because of the cost. It was almost a week before he consented and Shag saddled up "Dickie Boy," Betty's horse, riding off towards Anahim Lake late on a Friday afternoon.

The short fifty mile ride across the mountains was out of the question because of the deep snow, so he had to take the longer trail around. In bitter cold, 25 degrees below zero (F) during the day and slipping down to 50 below at night, plus bucking two feet of snow on the level and drifts that were higher, Shag and his horse were exhausted and cold when they arrived in town late Sunday afternoon. Due to inclement weather, it took two more days for Pat Carey to nurse his old Junkers from Quesnel out to Anahim Lake to meet Shag, who then flew out with him to show him which lake wasn't drifted over and safe to land on.

During the five days they waited for the plane, Pan lay motionless, with Betty, like a nurse, tending to his personal needs night and day.His only movement was when he had to use the makeshift bed pan she had contrived out of a tin. The slight change of position would put him in agonizing pain.

Again Pan was transported on the hay covered sleigh, when the plane arrived, each small bump in the trail still arousing pain that was plain hell for him. Loading him aboard the aircraft, which sat high off the ice, was another chore for all, but by using the cot again as a stretcher they finally got him settled in as comfortable as possible.

Carey flew Pan into Prince George, the flight directed there by the bad weather to the south. However, the Prince George doctors couldn't seem to do much for him and after a few days Pan became frustrated. He asked for a phone, then promptly called Alex Fraser, in Quesnel, to come and take him to the Quesnel General Hospital, "so Ole Doc Baker can take care of me right." Besides, he knew Alex's wife, Gertrude was the Hospital Matron there, and would keep an eye on him.

Alex made the trip in his station wagon the next day and managed to get Pan situated in the back, comfortably enough to withstand the 75 mile drive back to Quesnel. Once he was settled in the hospital, Doc Baker came right over. When he first examined Pan, all he could say was "Jesus." Pan's stomach looked like the colour of an eggplant, all reddish black and blue from the broken blood vessels.

After an x-ray and a thorough examination, Doctor Baker gave Pan the bad news. "Pan, I hate to tell you this, but when you came down hard on the edge of that trap you split the gristle in your groin and spread your pelvic bones. We're going to try traction, but I know you're a guy that would want it straight. I just don't think you'll ever walk again."

For the very first time, in his adult life, Pan shed a tear for himself. He turned his head away, tears in his eyes, but in a minute had himself under control and told Doc Baker, "I've got news for you. Yer wrong Doc. I WILL walk again! I've got a wife and kids out there at the ranch that won't make it if I don't get back. I've GOT to walk and ride again and BY GOD I WILL."

They kept Pan at the hospital, in the special traction, for a few months. The inactivity had him, mentally, climbing the walls, when in March word got to him that they were out of hay at the ranch. That did it. His grit and determination came to the fore, he had had it with being laid up in town. "Get me a plane, Alex. I'm going back home," he told his friend. Alex arranged for Tom Corliss, a local pilot, to fly him home, against Doc Baker's wishes.

Betty, Willie, Diana, Shag and Happy all welcomed him home with open arms. Pan, at once, took over the direction of the ranch, even though he couldn't participate, and directed the boys where to move the cattle to find fodder.

Happy, a born handyman, set up frames for a bed in the living room where Pan could be by the windows, the heater, and in the center of the family activities. Also, following Doc Baker's directions and drawings, he rigged up a traction device for Pan which they harnessed him into, again he was immobile. Betty had no explicit instructions for his care from the doctor, nor any way to consult with him, so she kept Pan tied into his rigging for a few months more.

On some days Pan would be in good spirits and talk about walking again. On other days, he would be depressed and felt it was useless to hope. Finally, on one of his 'down days,' Betty asked, "How do you know you'll never walk unless you try?"

The next day was an 'up' day for Pan. After thinking about it during the night, he had decided to give walking a try and when the boys came in for their noon meal, Pan called them over. "Shag, you and Happy come're a minute. Help me on my feet will ya?"

Pan seemed to get stronger immediately, after having made up his mind, that is until the boys helped him to his feet. Then his injury hurt so bad, he almost passed out, and his weakened legs shook so hard they had to lay him back on his bed, for fear he'd fall.

But Pan was a determined man once he had made up his mind, and from that moment, he was on his way back into the saddle. Every day he had the boys help him upright, each time standing a few minutes longer, and the pain a bit less, and after six weeks, he didn't need any help to stand.

Soon, he was able to sit in his favourite rocker. He had discovered too, that he could scoot himself about the house in it, making it to the dinner table, then pulling himself up on the bench, by hanging onto the table edge. This was a big help to Betty, she no longer had to take his meals into the living room for him.

After a spell of rocker activity, he got Shag and Happy to hold his arms while he attempted a couple of steps. It only took a short time until Betty could help him by herself.

RIDING A ROCKER INSTEAD OF A HORSE, and hating every minute of it. On nice days, when he was laid up, Pan liked to set out in the yard. Here he is shown with Betty and the children, Diana and "Willie" (Ken). In the background "Shag" Thompson is walking up to "Kitty Toy", who doesn't seem too appreciative of what's going to happen next.

Happy, the wood worker around the ranch, took on the task of making a pair of crutches for Pan. First he cut saplings, five feet long, splitting them two thirds of the way down. He next wrapped the whole lower part with moose hide thongs, laid a brace in above the thong wrapping where Pan's hands would be, thus seperating the two split sides. Next he measured Pan from his arm pits to the floor, cut the sides and laid in the top brace. By the time the thongs and sapplings had dried, the crutches were held tighter than if by glue. Pieces of an old tire were used for the tips. Betty sewed the arm pit paddings, laced them into place and Pan had as fine a pair of crutches as were ever made.

"I can't thank them boys enough," Betty told a neighbour later. "Shag would come in for breakfast, talk over the days chores with Pan, then get right to them; he took care of all the ranch and animals plus helping with Pan. Happy took over some of my work, like getting all the wood in and helped Shag too."

Pan nodded in agreement to her words. As Rich Boland, a young lad who came to the ranch later at age 17, said, "Pan never talked openly about his appreciation of a job well done, but you could tell he was appreciative by the way he acted."

Winter seemed longer than usual that year, but warm weather finally came and preparations were made to take Pan into Quesnel for a check up. Betty and the boys fixed a place for Pan in the wagon bed, making it as soft and comfortable as possible with hay and cushions. Since one of the boys needed to tend to the spring ranch work and keep an eye on Willie and Diana, Happy stayed behind, Shag going along to drive the team. It took them five days to make the trip. Being the marshes were still thawing and the bogs were already soft, they had to use the summer trail, avoiding the possibility of getting mired down yet made good time. Pan eased the bumps and jolts, as much as possible, by using his arms to steady himself.

At his clinic, Doc Baker gave Pan a thorough examination then had him go to the hospital for ex-rays. Suprised at what he found, Doc Baker told Pan, "It's hard for me to believe you've mended so well, you're pelvic bone is nearly back in place and your groin is almost healed. If you continue to take it easy, you'll be your old self in no time at all."

"Told ya so," was all Pan replied, chuckling.

Their next stop was at the Fraser store for supplies, they needed just about everything since it had been over a year since any large quantities had been freighted into the ranch. Alex was delighted his friend was back on his feet, even if it was with crutches. He, and Gertrude, wanted Pan and Betty to stay for a few days, but Betty fretted about the kids and Pan fretted about the spring ranch work, so they began the long journey home. Near Tibbles Lake, however, they stopped to see the Braydens. There they were pressed into staying, Buster insisting they had to celebrate

Bob and Eileen Paley's and Wallace and Betty Paley's double wedding reception.

Upon hearing about the party, neither Pan nor Betty could refuse,they had been confined too long at the ranch not to take advantage of seeing old friends,and "whooping it up a little."

The party started early, then ended up on Brayden's outside dance floor. The C.C., with a shot of home brew for a chaser now and then, endowed Pan with a fine rosy glow. Betty and Lizzie Paley were tapping their toes to the fiddler's happy music along side him. Both seemed to come up with the same idea at the same time, they laid Pan's crutches down, each grabbed an arm and out on the dance floor they went, all the while Pan insisting he couldn't get along without his crutches. But before long, taken up with the dancers, he forgot all about them.

The next morning, Pan awoke yelling, "Betty, get my sticks, I gotta make a quick trip to the outhouse!"

"Can't find them anyplace," she scolded. "You shouldn't have given them away, to God only knows who, last night--Doc Baker didn't say anything about you trotting around without them."

Not able to locate his crutches or find out who Pan had so generously 'given' them to the night before, Pan hobbled around while Betty packed up; and they resumed their trip home, after their good-byes were said.

Pan sent Willie looking for sticks with a crook on one end, promptly upon their arrival at the Home Ranch. Willie soon found two that suited Pan just fine and with his pocket knife, he proceeded to 'whittle' them into a reasonable resemblance of canes. Using these, Pan then resumed his exercise walks.

Mid-June rolled around and all conversation turned to the upcoming Anahim Lake Stampede, considered as the family's yearly holiday. Since Pan was so much better it was decided that they would go.

On July 2nd, they hit the trail for Anahim Lake, the kids on horseback, Pan and Betty on the wagon with Pan doing the driving. He took only one cane, not wanting to look too decrepit around town.

At the rodeo, and later at the dance, Pan's glow, from the 'welcome out' drinks, was gaining momentum, he was getting cagier by the minute at walking with only one cane. An old native man, more inebrieated than Pan staggered across the dance floor. Pan took one look and said, "Here you take this. You need it worse than I do," and walked off leaving the old Indian standing there holding the cane, wondering what the hell it was all about. Then, even through his alcohol dulled mind, the native caught the meaning of the gift, as he saw Pan grab Betty about the waist and whirl her onto the dance floor. Almost in unison, the other dancers stepped back, joined hands in a circle and cheered the couple on.

After the dance was over, Pan walked back to their camp by himself, but the next morning he was so stiff that he couldn't get out of his bedroll. He roused most of the camp, bellowing at Betty, "Wher-in-hell's my cane?" Like the crutches, it was never seen again.

Betty and the kids, figured the old Indian would discard it right outside the dance hall, but the cane wasn't to be found. D'arcy Christensen and Bob Smith, two friends, joined the search, came up empty handed, but later managed to scrounge up another one from the dark recesses of D'arcy's store.

Meantime, Pan had been cooling his heels, sitting on a stump by the campfire. "Didn't think I'd get so damned drunk I'd give away my third leg," he lamented.

During the long fall and winter, Pan became adept at easing his way to the corrals and outbuildings by using the cane. Little by little, he put less dependency on it and he thought about riding again. Word got around, via the moccasin telegraph, that Pan Phillips was just about ready to fork a horse once more. There was silent cheering in the Blackwater and Chilcotin by his friends. As a result an anonymous friend sent Pan a gift with a note.

"You sure as hell can't fork a horse right off, so here's an old side saddle my old lady will never need again. You try that for a spell before you do something stupid and get yourself back into that harness rig."

Pan wished he could thank the donor, but allowed he probably didn't want his wife to know he had given her saddle away. He was grateful and could hardly wait to try it out. The saddle worked perfectly, so much so in fact that Pan was able to run the trap line for the rest of the winter.

The following summer, Pat sat asrtide Old Whitney in a standard saddle, for the first time in over two years. He discovered he could ride comfortably, though when walking he still used a cane. Then it, too, joined the pile of discarded rigging and Pan was back riding tall in the saddle.

"Pan was the best shot I've ever seen. With his 44 S&W six-shooter, he made Jessie James look like a school teacher."

———Leo Lillienwise

DEAD EYE FROM WYOMING

Many of the people interviewed for this book testified to the fact that Pan Phillips was undoubtly one of the best shots with a six gun that ever lived. Some people are born with a knack for shooting and Pan was one, while others go through life unable to hit a barn door, regardless of practice.

We've been told of Pan sticking matches in a tree and lighting them with a shot; of shooting the heads off three grouse in rapid succession; of outshooting a Mountie, enlarging the holes in a can the Mountie had hit with his rifle bullets; and on and on, adinfinitum. However, admitedly, Pan didn't always engage his brains before shooting. He was so sure of himself, and the gun in his hand, that he was known to throw discretion to the wind on occasion.

Once Betty, while cleaning house, picked up a shoe box with a little hole in the end and heard a mouse inside. She ran out the door, box in hand, asking Pan to get rid of the mouse. Instantly he obliged. He pulled his well used Smith and Wesson (which he always wore in earlier days) and placed a shot through the box in Betty's hand. It dispatched the mouse. There is no doubt but what the rodents demise was 100% sheer luck, but Pan took credit for knowing just where the mouse would be in the box by the way Betty carried it and took credit for a planned shot.

To say Betty was upset would be putting it midly.

D'arcy Christensen tells of one time in his store, when he swatted at a fly. Pan was in town and standing close by. D'arcy missed the fly that lit on the window. "I'll take care of him," Pan said, whipped out his six shooter and shot it. Naturally D'arcy's window went out with the fly. By the time D'arcy rounded up some glass to fix the window, he found a jaybird sitting on top of his cash register, it having flown through the void left by Pan's over exuberance. We never did find out if Pan paid for the window.

CLOWNING AROUND. Pan, with foot on "Cash box", joins three other 'desperadoes' for a picture. The varience in names given for the other three lead to them being dubbed "unidentified". Apparently the top hat worn by one was Pan's and was a prop for his humourous antics for some time. The six shooter strapped to the second man reportedly was Pan's gun that made him famous as a marksman. No clues were given as to the rifle ownership, or history, nor to the knife in the other man's mouth.

Willie was given a watch and when it quit working he laid it on the living room table, turned to his Dad and asked him if he could fix it. Again Pan acted on impulse. "Sure, I'll fix it," he said, pulled his gun and shot the watch. It ricocheted off the table, right through the living room window, shattering the glass, much to Pan's surprise and Willie's consternation.

Betty may not have been at a loss for words over this incident, but she was at a loss as how to explain Pan's actions to Willie.

On one freight trip to Anahim Lake, Pan arrived at his friends, Harold and Alyce Engebretson's place, tired and hungry. He found Harold outside in the yard, scratching his head looking up into a tree at a hind quarter of a moose hanging there. In the days before refrigeration and freezers, meat was often pulled up high to keep it from getting fly blown, since a fly will only go 25 ft. above the ground.

"Time for supper. Can't get the damned meat down. Rope's jumped the pulley," Harold announced in his slow inimitable way.

"Nothin to it," Pan said as he drew his six-shooter. One well placed bullet and the meat fell to the ground. He had cut the 1/4 inch thick rope, 30 feet up in the tree with the one shot. Harold stood there amazed.

"Shortened yer rope up a couple of feet, but what the hell, let's eat." Pan said.

We could go on with other tales about Pan and his six shooter, but we think we have made our point. Pan's reactions to any given situation was unpredictable.

Little was said about his marksmanship with a rifle, until we interviewed Pan's close friend, Ed Adams, who had this story to tell us.

Seems Pan and he were way down to the far end of the big meadow at the Home Ranch getting up hay for stacking, when they looked back up the meadow at a big finished stack, to see a bull moose standing on his hind legs, with both front feet on the top rail of the pole fence grabbing big mouthsfull of hay and munching contentedly.

"Watch me put a scare into that freeloader," Pan grumbled as he grabbed his rifle and began putting on a show for Ed. He tested the wind with a wet finger, sighted up the meadow at eye level first, then gradually lifted up the rifle muzzle, as though he was aiming at a flock of geese. "That oughta do it," he said as he pulled the trigger on the impossible shot, the moose being at least a quarter of a mile away.

The sound of the shot reverberated off the fringe of spruce trees around the meadow. The big bull appeared to shudder as it jumped down and ran around behind the hay stack. Pan "Hee hee"-ed, put his gun back and continued loading the hay rack on the sleigh, after a few calming words to his team. When the sleigh was almost loaded, Pan told Ed to finish it off and bring it down to the far stack while he had a look around behind to check on the moose.

When Ed finally drove up to the stack, and walked around behind, he found Pan busy skinning out the moose. With one chance in a thousand of hitting it from that distance, Pan had managed to aim so that his slug hit the moose right in the back, severing the spine. It was already dead when it walked behind the stack, it just didn't know it yet.

"Well, I'll be damned," was all Ed could say.

"Nothin' to it, boy. Ya jist gotta figure wind drift and range for a shot like that." Pan said with a twinkle in his eye, as if he never doubted his marksmanship for a moment.

We will have to agree with Ed and give Pan less credit for skill than luck, on that shot.

One other time a raven had taken a shine to berries in Betty's garden and had become a pest. Pan sitting in the living room, looked out through the kitchen window, saw the culprit on the garden fence post, grabbed a 22 calibre rifle and dispatched the raven, the bullet traveling through the kitchen between Diana and her mother and through the glass in the kitchen window.

Fortunately being of small calibre, the bullet didn't shatter the glass. It did, however, shatter Betty's nerves and we're sure you don't have the time to sit here and read all she had to say to Pan regarding his reckless shot.

"Pan's camps at the stampede were always strictly - no
frills."

——Alan "Shag" Thompson

HOT DOGS AND OVER PROOF RUM

Pan's social activities centered around the parties
held at the end of each cattle drive, the cattle auction in
Quesnel that followed and the Anahim Lake Stampede.
The latter being the source of his family's main yearly
outing and enjoyment. The stampede coupled with some of
his other 'in town' activities that have been noted herein,
made him an unforgetable leading character in the history
of Anahim Lake.

Pan took an active part in the business function of the
early stampedes and was a real booster for the cattlemen's
association. Once in town, he seemed to come across far
more opportunities for pranks than he could cope with and
certainly hated to miss a chance for some fun.

One year the stampede committee found itself facing
a financial problem. They hadn't been breaking even and
something had to be done. The rodeo being dear to Pan's
heart, he and D'arcy Christensen put their heads together
and made the committee an offer they couldn't refuse.
They agreed to pay a set figure each year, on a five year
contract, for the food concession at the stampede grounds.
That would take all the guess work and risk off the
committee's hands, they would know exactly what income
they could expect from the stand. The deal was struck.

Came the stampede time and Pan rode in from the
ranch well in advance. D'arcy and he spent considerable
time burning the midnight oil, planning their first season
as consessionaires while searching for the bottom of a
couple bottles of O.P. rum in the process. Finally, they
agreed on their food list, but another problem faced them.
There was no refrigeration available. "So how can we get
the meat in advance and then keep it from spoiling?"
D'arcy asked.

"Same damned way we do stuff out home. We'll dig us a
cooler pit right in the middle of the stand and when we
need meat we'll jist reach down and grab some."

"Helluva an idea," D'arcy replied.

The next few days saw Pan and him getting a little exercise digging the pit, then building a wooden top for it. Came the day before the big wild west rodeo, campout, dance, singout and knockout was to begin. A truck from town rolled in with all their foodstuffs, backed up to the stand and unloaded. When it came to the meat and buns, Pan raised the wooden lid and let out a howl like a coyote with it's paw in a trap.

D'arcy ran over to see what had Pan so riled up. Some of the expletives he used would have melted the shoes off a horse. "Some son-of-a-bitch crapped in our cooler pit!" he said at the end of his tirade. Whether the person did it as a joke, or was drunk, they had themselves a problem.

"What the hell do we do now? You ain't getting me down there to shovel it out," vowed Pan.

"I got kinda a weak stomach myself,"

"Gimme that damned shovel. I'll take care of it."
Pan began hastily shoveling dirt in on top of the mess.

"Whatcha gonna do?"

"Bury it - what the hell else? Ain't gonna hurt nothing if you guys keep your yaps shut." Pan shot a baleful look at the truck driver which found it's mark.

The net result was that nice tasty hamburger meat and buns came out of the cooler for the full three days, no one but Pan and D'arcy was the wiser and people remarked about their delicious flavor. This may be the first time the story has been told.

Pan had a few tricks up his sleeve to cut down expenses at the stand. Milk cans had only one hole punched in them, 'packer style' he called it, but in reality it made it very hard to shake the cream out. With customers lined up for coffee, few put too much effort in getting the cans to produce. The net result was a saving of several cans of milk.

Pan, also, saw to it that all coffee cups were filled right to the brim. "Coffee costs less than cream and sugar," he figured. "If you don't leave them much room to add it, they won't use as much."

So it was that for five years Pan and D'arcy stood shoulder to shoulder handing out pop, hot dogs, hamburgers, coffee, sweets and snoose to the stampede crowd, aided by assistants, Ann McKilvington, the Anahim Lake school teacher, and others.

But Pan always wondered if he had slipped up somewhere. He never did figure out how to control the amount of mustard customers could plaster on their hot dogs. He tried using the smallest plastic spoons made, but then there was usually some cowpoke who would come along, whip out his hunting knife, jam it in the jar and really load up the bun. "Can't win them all," Pan figured.

Pan, with his expertise on riding, was a stampede arena director occasionally. There too, he presented the typical cowboy image - dressed in boots, jeans, chaps and sweat stained Stetson. He rode like he and the horse were one, the last man you would expect to see get bucked off.

Pan reveled in the image he portrayed and usually rode his most sure footed horse when he was judging, hazing or riding before the spectators.

In 1959, during the annual Director's race, Pan on a borrowed mount, and his cohorts were going all out, their horses in a dead run, when a sudden movement in the crowd caught his horse's eye and it shied instantly without giving Pan any indication by a flex of it's muscles or a turn of it's head. The movement was so sudden that Pan litterally was left sitting in air to the right of his horse. He hit the ground hard and his ego went down with him.

The crowd roared, whistled and clapped. They had seen their hero bite the dust. Pan got up, knocked the dust off, caught his horse and just grinned. "Everyone bites the dust sooner or later and I guess it was just my time," he told one of the fellows who had run out to see if he was okay. "Nothin' broken and feelin' fine," assured Pan, but not quite telling the truth. He didn't ride again that day.

By the next morning, Pan was really in pain and Betty had to send Diana for Dr. Alex Holley, while Pan grumbled about, "Let's not spread the word. Don't want the whole damned country to know I'm gimped up."

Doc was finally rousted out of his tent and came over to examine Pan, discovering that he had re-seperated his pelvis, it still being weak from the previous injury. So Doc Holley had to come up with some old fashioned, pioneer ingenuity, because Pan insisted on carrying on with his rodeo duties. No way was anyone going to keep him in his tent.

Alex called a gathering of the clan and told them what he needed; a big, old, tough, truck tire innertube and he didn't give a damn where they found one. The search was on and it wasn't long before one appeared, source unknown. From the tube he cut a strip of rubber the right length to go around Pan's hips, then sent someone else to appropriate a pair of long, leather boot laces from D'arcy's store, while he cut eyelets along the edge of his makeshift rubber contrivance.

With everything ready, he had Betty help him and they placed the rubber around Pan's hips, over his underwear, then Doc laced it up, "just like putting a corset on a woman," which pulled the seperation together. Someone else had borrowed a pair of crutches and when the rodeo started Pan was out in the arena, hobbling about. The 'girdle' didn't seem to bother him any and he took the inconvenience and jesting in his stride. When the stampede was over, Pan returned the crutches had his wagon loaded with freight, and drove the fifty miles back to the Home Ranch, still wearing the rubber gizmo.

Doc Holley wasn't sure how long Pan wore the contraption, but the next time he had a chance to check Pan over his pelvis seemed to have repaired itself again as good as could be expected, and Pan was ready for new adventures.

Since Pan was not one to let any opportunity to have a little fun pass by strangers too could easily find themselves the brunt of a prank.

At the stampede one year, the Phillip's family was camped down below the Dean River store, their camp surrounded by countless others. Liquor flowed like water, people sang, B.S.ed and as usual enjoyed the once a year gathering of friends as it were.

A young fellow, obviously from the city, had discovered that these ranchers, natives, and cattlemen were more than generous with their booze so he was flitting from camp to camp looking for free drinks. After making many stops, he filtered into the ring around the Phillip's campfire and never missed a swig when the jug was passed. It wasn't long before he fell off the log in a stupor and thus the stage was set for another Pan Phillips' gag.

Pan rustled around in the wagon, found hammer and nails, came back, removed the laced type oxfords from the man's feet, and without any comment, nailed them to the butt end of the log. Then he casually drug the drunk up to the log and laced his feet back into his shoes. Pan retired back to the fire waiting for the obvious to happen.

Around midnight, the cold night air brought the panhandling drunk to, and he tried to move. The singing and talking came to an abrupt halt as all eyes riveted on the man's attempts to move his legs, the futile attempts bringing him out of his stupor. Finally, he raised his head, saw his shoes attached to the log and realized he'd been the butt of a joke. He quickly unlaced his shoes, pulled his feet out of them and in his stocking feet, drifted into the darkness. No one in camp ever saw him again.

Obviously, Pan's hoax was one of the highlights of that trek to the stampede.

Doc Holley and Lester Dorsey had been the brunt of Pan's pranks since they had met him, and few were the times they had gotten even. But one year at the stampede, they found a bit of inspiration in a jug of C.C. and followed up on it.

Early one morning, after the campfires, singing, yelling and yahooing had quieted down, the whole Phillips tribe rolled up into their bedrolls inside their tent (the same one used on the beef drives). Lester and Doc crept up outside. Both got a good hold of opposite end posts and on a nod from Lester gave a tug. The ridge pole and tent collapsed on the sleeping figures. Pandemonium broke out under the flattened canvas.

Lester couldn't control imself and began cackling. Betty, awake and fire coming out of her eyes, heard him, recognizing his voice. What she said we'll omit here, gentle reader, but suffice it to say, it put wings on Lester's feet and he lit out. Doc stayed to gloat, as heads began to appear out of other tent flaps and racous laughter, at Pan's come-up-ance, engulfed the campground.

The highlight of the 1961 stampede, for Pan, was the fun of showing off his son Homer, visiting from Wyoming; introducing him to his friends and initiating him into the Canadian wild and wooly west. Homer's month long stay was packed with adventure each day, Pan made sure of that.

Pan made an attempt to attend as many of the annual Anahim Lake Cattleman's Association meetings as possible, and for a time, served as a director. The meeting dates were set for the third Saturday in May and the third Saturday in November. To attend these meetings, Pan went in on horseback, leading pack horses. Both dates were in uncertain enough weather between sleigh and wagon traveling that he was afraid of getting caught and then not getting his supplies back home.

While serving his directorship, he made it in early one time to attend the executive meeting, held prior to the open general meeting. There it was brought out that the association was financially embarrassed, and needed to prod some of the non-current attending members into coughing up their membership dues.

Pan normally had little to say, concerning the association's operation, but this turn of events, he thought, would give him a chance to be seen and heard. Besides, he wholeheartedly believed in the need for the organization. He rose to the occasion in grand style, inundating those present with numerous reasons why they should bring their dues up to date in support of the association.

In the middle of his tirade, the treasurer, who had missed the executive meeting and just arrived, jumped to his feet and called out, "Now jist a gol danged minute there Phillips. Why don't you practice what yer preachin'? Yer damn dues ain't paid neither."

Pan sat down, red faced. The members roared. His only excuse, hastily thought up, was that he thought Betty had sent in his cheque.

> "Pan couldn't stop B.S.ing long enough to eat properly.
> He talked like a machine gun, with his mouth full."
> ——Richard Boland

PASS THE GRUB

Pan was a meat and potatoes man, basically, but also, had a taste for the goodies. Before each meal he would ask, "What's fer dessert?" because he wanted to save room. He really wasn't fussy about his food, and under some circumstances sat down to pretty strange concoctions, like hog jowls and cabbage for a week straight one time when Betty was in town.

The Phillip's family, and crew, never ate beef. That was saved for the market. Moose, venison, bear, ducks, geese, and occasionally caribou were their main courses. They didn't eat muskrat or beaver, as did many of their neighbours. Nor did Pan, or any of the people in the area, eat horse meat. "Too much like eatin' yer friend," Pan would say.

During the war years, when most staples were rationed, and two weeks supply of sugar was the allowance, Pan had to go before the board and get a permit to buy more than that, as he normally freighted in groceries only twice a year. When in town he bartered meat, butter and gasoline ration stamps for unused liquor stamps. Pan discovered a real source of supply among the clergy in town.

"HABA—CURE," a product Pan sold at the ranch store, was used to cure their meat. Moose cured with it made a good substitute for bacon.

Pan loved moose fat. "White meat," he called it. In the summer, a young bull moose would have two to three inches of fat on the meat and Pan could down a half dozen, half meat-half fat, steaks at a sitting. His breakfast fare was invariably moose steak and pancakes. His favourite snacks were dried fruit, cheese and crackers and peanut butter, which he ate by the spoonfuls.

He washed his breakfast down with tea, as did most of the old timers, and drank coffee with the rest of his meals. When traveling by himself, Pan took very little in the way of food with him, relying on his six shooter or 22 rifle for spruce hens to go along with the cheese, smoked meat, tea and crackers.

When hunting, Pan took special care of the meat after the animal was shot and it always turned out good. No food was wasted. He knew just how to cut up an animal to avoid waste and what did get left over was used to feed the dogs and cats.

To a man, the ex-ranch hands who worked for Pan on the Home Ranch, reported the food was plentiful and tasty. There was the odd time when supplies would get low, but most of the time they ate well. The main evening meal was followed by dessert, sometimes canned fruit.

No one thought it odd that often several cans would be set on the table without labels. When queried about them, Pan passed it off as the tins getting wet and the labels falling off; or the labels knocked off during the long trail ride; or even that the damned rats chewed them off. His answers always seemed reasonable and appeased them, but the hit and miss method of fruit selection left something to be desired.

If one of the hands liked cherries, sure as hell he'd pick a can with apricots, or if he liked plums, he'd unerringly pick one containing applesauce. On the other hand, Pan dearly loved peaches and it seemed uncanny the way his unlabled can usually turned out to be full of peaches. Happy Thompson set himself to thinking about this situation. It just didn't add up. There was too much of a co-incidence in Pan always getting what he liked, so Happy set out to find the answer.

One evening Happy beat Pan and the other hands into the house for supper, then hid behind a door to watch. Sure enough, Pan was taking labels off the cans, studying each can's markings closely and memorizing the contents by fly specks, glue marks, dents, the numbers on the bottom, and any other tell tale signs, making sure that he positively had the peach cans pegged. Happy knew then that they had all been hoodwinked for months.

Christmas was a time of year, when Pan showed his family more attention than usual. He'd hitch up the sleigh and they'd all go for a ride into the sparser thicket, towards the mountains, in search of that 'just right' tree. It would be brought back to the house and decorated with an assortment of home made and boughten ornaments which had been added to, year by year.

Pan tried to get into Anahim Lake mid-December, returning home before Christmas so the kids would have their presents on time. On those occasions, it added to the spirit of the season, as the kids sat for hours wondering what was in this package or that one. Because of weather his trip was delayed until January, then they celebrated a late holiday. Christmas dinner, however, was prepared on time, because Pan's freight sleigh in November would yield up a turkey, sweet potatoes, cranberries, 'store bought' candy, mince meat, and pumpkin for pie. Betty was "no slouch as a cook," and the meal would be scrumptious, long remembered during the following months of ranch grub (moose meat and spuds) ahead.

Once in awhile the holiday season brought another pleasant suprise in an unexpected visitor. One such year it was Andy Holte, who showed up just a few days after Christmas, his sleigh loaded with four boxes of Japanese oranges, a box of apples, and a pair of skis for each of the kids. Andy Holte was like that. A man that truly enjoyed doing something for others. He would spend time with his own family, then leave them for a few days, or weeks, while he was off on some errand of good will, such as his Home Ranch visit. Andy was indeed a very good friend to have, Pan knew.

As we mentioned, Pan liked his goodies and one thing he dearly loved was ice cream. In later years when at the fishing camp, as his taste for this delicacy became known, more and more customers brought it in with them just to watch him devour it in great quantities. He could sit down, eat half a gallon, burp, and reach for more. Next to ice cream was rhubarb pie, cream pies and fresh applesauce as desserts.

Marshmallows were another favourite. He kept them stashed in the kitchen cupboards, nooks and crannies. When the grandkids came, he'd share with them, but only after they had hid their eyes so they couldn't see his hiding places.

When Pan was alone, he would take any short cuts possible with cooking and end up putting some strange meals on the table. Floyd Vaughan once landed to find Pan finishing off a breakfast of boiled cabbage and mutton tallow. When invited to join him, Floyd declined.

Pan, also drank a lot of milk when they had a milk cow, otherwise he resorted to powered milk. While visiting Diana and his son-in-law, Barry, he would drink fresh milk by the quart, perhaps to quiet his queasy stomach which he acquired along the line.

He loved spicy food but in later years, it didn't love him. He bought Tums by the case. After eating his fill of a dish he knew wasn't going to agree with him, he would pull out the Tums, trying to get a jump on his acidity. He would often eat so many that he would get a white streak running down from the corners of his mouth, and not notice until someone would say, "Better go rinse off your kisser, Pan."

After Pan had a propane refrigerator blow up, he stopped serving food in the fishing camp lodge and let customers bring in 'their own grub' to cook for themselves in each cabin. It was like Christmas to him when they departed for then he would scurry over to the vacated cabin to see what food they had left, lugging it over to his own kitchen. Like a squirrel, he stored it for another day.

Pan was a well muscled man, but when he left the Home Ranch's heavy chores behind he began to put on fat and flab. When he really had a paunch around his middle, he elected to try a grapefruit diet. Later, he told Bill Solowoniuk that he had to give it up. He had passed out four times and just couldn't get full, so he went back to eating meat. As far as we could learn, it was the only time he tried out one of the fad diets.

"Pan Phillips left behind a legacy of caring for people, animals, and nature."

————Alex Fraser

FOUR FOOTED FRIENDS

On an average over the years, Pan kept anywhere from 20 to 30 horses on the ranch and at his fishing camp. Another book could be written for horse lovers, on the personalities, misfortunes and the hands that rode them. We have touched on but a few of them in this book.

Several of Pan's horses became known by name throughout the Chilcotin and Blackwater areas. "Old Whitey" was one such horse. Pan raised him from a colt and his exploits on the trail are legend.

When Old Whitey was a colt, Pan would use his mother, teamed with another horse, to pull the hay rake and not wanting the colt tagging along in the way, he would lock it up in the corral where it would whinney mournfully. Sooner or later the kids would begin to feel sorry for him, take the colt to the ranch house yard, and let it run. And run it would, right in the front door and out the back door, once in awhile leaving it's calling card on the living room floor. That would end the romp for that day, as Betty outvoted the kids and the colt went back to the corral.

Perhaps the names of other. now famous horses in Pan Phillips' string won't mean much to you, but to others who will read this book, each name will bring back a memory, not only of Pan, but of a horse with it's own personality that did something outstanding to make people remember it.

"Little Alec," "Dickey Boy," "Trooper," "Paratrooper," "Smokey," "Nimpo," "Scotty," "Buster," "Pearl," and of course "Old Whitey," were the best known of the herd. When Pan spoke of them, it was as if he was talking about a friend, always calling the horse by name.

Pan usually topped off (gentling them so another rider might stay on their back) the horses himself, "just to take the rough edges off," before giving it to one of the green hands to ride. He would tell them, "You don't know nothing, this horse don't know nothing, so you'll both learn together."

A YOUNG COLT gets a steadying hand from Pan.
Photo taken in Sept. of 1956.

"Pan could shoe any horse that drew the breath of life,"
Ed Adams told us. And often he had to prove it on the trail.

Pan was more soft hearted about his animals than
people thought. He knew when to be firm and rough with
them and when to be gentle, for their sake and his own.
Inwardly, he was glad that they never had to slaughter too
many animals themselves.

On one cattle drive, Rob began kidding about the
cattle not knowing where they were going (meaning the
slaughterhouse) and Pan revealed his soft heart by telling
Rob, "Shut up, that ain't funny." It was a quick peek into his
father's inner feelings Rob had never seen before.

Some horses and cattle naturally became pets along
with the usual assortment of dogs and cats, but the Home
Ranch, also, had an unusual addition to the pet menagerie,
a big, boar hog that got so tame it would follow everyone
and anyone while doing their chores, including Ed Adams
on the hay rake making long, numerous swaths up and
down the meadow. When a plane would land on the
airstrip, the pig would dash across the meadow to greet
the new arrivals. It then proceeded to inspect the plane and
people with accompaning oinks, grunts and loud sniffing
as if to make sure they were okay.

However, the hog came to an untimely end due to his
insistance of chewing up everything it could get into it's
mouth, edible or not. One visitor to the ranch laid his fairly
new saddle on the front porch out of the rain. The hog
enjoyed the leather thongs. Quite tasty. Jackie and Albert
Tossoff from Mud River, rode in to visit for a few days and
Jackie laid her new, leather chaps on the porch. The
leather that was left wouldn't have made a pair of chaps for
a midget.

That did it. Pan and the family had had enough
apologizing to do.

Ham, anyone?

Another animal well remembered, was a big ram
sheep that Ed Adams had bought. It turned out to be the
"buttingest and horniest ram west of the Rockies."
Unafraid, it would back up, put it's head down and butt
anything that moved - bulls, horses, cows, people, dogs and
probably would have taken on a grizzly bear if it had the
chance. Being raised around mostly cattle, the ram became

somewhat confused and would try to breed any heifer laying down. Pan thought this was hilarious and often wondered what the outcome would have been if the ram had succeeded.

One fall, as they started their annual beef drive to Quesnel, Pan was amazed to find the ram mixed in with the cattle strung out along the trail. That night when they camped at Paul Meadow, he locked the ram in a barn at the nearest Indian's place, instructing the natives to let it out after the cattle were a couple days down the trail. Pan figured it would then return to the ranch. However, the ram had other ideas, that night it butted down the barn door. Next morning Pan again found it mixed with the cattle ready to hit the trail. That did that. Pan lassoed the animal, drug it back to the barn, tied the ram up inside, and nailed the door shut. When he got back from Quesnel...you guessed it.

Lamb Chops, anyone?

Betty, Diana and the boys got to know each of their own calves so well that they not only had them named, they could tell you which bull bred which heifer, dates of birth, sickness and the treatments, at what weight the animal was sold, the price it brought and it's offspring, if it produced any. Betty occasionally allowed the kids to bring a calf into the house to play, but at the first sign of a raised tail out it went.

There was a period of time when British Columbia's back country was infested with American draft dodgers (hippies) and the Blackwater was no exception. Pan tolerated them, but deep down as an ex-yank, he resented their attitudes toward the U.S., but avoided discussion on the subject.

One day two of them, from a camp on Tsacha Lake, came through the fishing camp on horseback on their way to the Home Ranch long after Pan had sold it. They stopped for a cup of coffee, then rode on. Later in the early morning hours they rode back into the fishing camp and while Pan slept soundly, Gayle, who was working for her Dad at the time, gave the men a cabin and went back to bed.

Along about six a.m. Pan awoke, dressed and went outside. He saw the horses tied to the hitching rail. When he noted that they were still saddled, and their cinches had never been loosened, it loosened up his tongue. Waking Gayle, he found what cabin the two men were in and stomped over to it to actually boot them out of their bunks. "If yer gonna live in this country, you damned well better learn that your animals come first when it comes time to bed down." After he had cooled down he had Gayle feed them breakfast, then sent them on their way. It is a reasonably fair bet that they never left their horses cinched up tight again after Pan 'dressed them down.'

The winter of 1976, was a very sad time for Pan. It was a hard cruel winter with too much snow for the horses (which by then were the only animals he had) to rustle up feed. To add to their plight, the earlier spring had been wet and the hay yield had not been up to par. Diana and Barry and Pan faced the prospect of having their older and weaker horses die of starvation that winter.

It was one of the hardest decisions Pan ever had to make. He, and Barry, finally decided they would rather shoot the horses than to see them slowly starve. Pan couldn't bring himself to do the actual shooting, so Barry had the miserable task. Fifteen horses went down that day and Pan stood by the fence unashamedly crying, especially when Old Whitey dropped. Into each man's life some rain must fall, it's said. It poured on Pan Phillips that day and it took a while for him to get back to being his cheerful self again.

"Dad (Pan) was my idol, because he personified the western life I liked."

——Gayle Phillips Simpson

GETTING TO KNOW HIM

By now you may have formulated an idea of your own, as to Pan's disposition and personality, which, many admitted, was complex.

Perhaps, we should take time here to clarify a few points so that you can get a clearer picture of the man. The following passages may give you a better insight into the character and the thinking of Pan Phillips.

Pan came into the country with a few set ideas of his own about ranching and packing, but he was smart enough to be able to adapt them to the Chicotin and Blackwater terrain and climate. Intestinal fortitude carried him through the hard times after the Frontier Cattle Company folded. Any lesser man would have given up, but not Pan. He was determined to carry on with his dream. Ultimately, it did pay off for him, not so much in monetary wealth as it did in self satisfaction.

His financial affairs were kept in good order and he did not overspend. He also did a fair job of bookeeping. Once he caught the bank in a seven cent error and could hardly wait to get into town to "give 'em hell."

And he wasn't much of a gambler. "Too cussed tight, fraid he might lose five cents," more than one person told us. It appears, however, he did get enticed into a game of poker with two friends, Wes Carter and D'arcy Christenson, the results catastrophic by Pan's standards. He lost a hundred dollars. "That's the first, last and only time, you kin bet yer rump on that," he told D'arcy.

D'arcy had met Pan when he was very young, and perhaps, through the years had gotten to know him as well as anyone in the country. "Pan wouldn't venture a dime, unless the odds were highly in his favor. He could squeeze a nickle until the beaver crapped."

During the war years, the Pacific Rangers were formed; it was a group of volunteers who filled in for the lack of police and military protection in remoter B.C. areas. In general, the volunteers kept an eye out for any unusual or criminal activity and acted as spotters for possible enemy planes. They were especially alert after a Japanese submarine was sighted, surfaced, in the Bella Coola bay.

Pan was approached and agreed to become a ranger, however, there is no known encounter that necessitated action on his part. As a ranger Pan was furnished ammunition and with this free bonanza, he kept his guns oiled up as well and his marksmanship on target. He did his bit for his adopted country, being 'frozen' to his ranch by wartime decree.

Our research showed that Pan was a good drinking man. His favourite drink was 'anything,' as long as it was free. He did prefer CC and water, or on occasion he would have it with 7-Up, but hardly anything else, ever. When he got into a bottle of rum, he would use Coke as a mixer if it was available.

Reports of the parties he's held or attended, are legend and always the image appeared of him being a two fisted drinker. Yet, few people said they ever actually saw Pan 'knock-down-drag-out' drunk. We did hear of one occasion, however, where booze took over common sense and the results gave the entire Blackwater "a helluva laugh."

Pan had come into Anahim Lake, after the fall cattle drive and, as usual, he and his good friend Lester Dorsey got together. It wasn't a question of whether or not there would be a party, just how many days it would last. However, their plans and the party were destined to terminate a bit early this time, as they ran out of liquor near midnight the first night. A couple of the partygoers were sent out to replenish the supply, but upon returning later, reported that they had rousted out everybody they knew and not a drop was to be had. Anahim Lake was dry.

"Well, we ain't about to quit now," Pan avowed. "We'll jist run down to Williams Lake for a case or two. That Jeep of yours runnin', Lester? "

"Hell, yes! Let's go!"

The two traipsed out, Pan grabbing the one bottle containing a few shots, leaving the rest to continue the party without them. They climbed into Lester's old, dilapidated, ex-army jeep, ignoring the fact that Williams Lake was over 200 miles away and a long, long, days drive. They were two shinning knights off to salvage the party.

And it didn't register with them, either, that the roads were icy and it was snowing flakes bigger than 'duck droppings.'

"God damned lights ain't working," Lester declared.

"To hell with them. It'll be daylight in a few hours, and in the meantime, I'll jist open the door on my side and tell you when you get too close to the ditch and you watch on yer side."

It didn't take long before the snow and cold began to dim the glow the liquor had built in them and Pan started to take serious thought of the situation, as the jeep careened from side to side down the narrow road barely missing the ditch each time.

"Hey, stop this damned thing! I kin see some sorta light out there, maybe I can get the lights to workin' better."

Lester hit the brakes and the jeep skidded sideways down the road before coming to a stop. Pan got out to take a look.

"Jesus Christ, Lester, you forgot to put the God damned hood down." Pan slammed it shut.

"Christ, that's a helluva lot better. Get back in, times awasting."

There is no accurate record of how many more miles they actually went before the bottle got completely dry and the booze wore off, but it is known that either the snow, cold, sobriety, or common sense, or a combination of all four, came over them somewhere between Nimpo Lake and Kleena Kleene. They returned to Anahim Lake to find the party defunct.

As Happy Thompson put it, "Pan had a magnetic personality. When he came into a room, where the party was dead, it soon would come to life. When he left a lively party, it soon would die."

Another episode with Lester, occured when Pan, Hod and Larry Smith, and he were indulged in a 'bull session' outside of town a ways, when Paul St. Pierre, author of "Chilcotin Holiday," came by and naturally joined in. Paul opened his car trunk, took out a bottle of CC and offered them all a drink. Pan reached first, removed the top, threw it as far as he could and said, "We sure as hell won't need that again." And they didn't.

Pan took far more note of his own birthday than most men. Knowing this the family always made plans for some sort of celebration, and for his 50th, they decided to get him away from the ranch. They hitched up a team and sleigh and set out for Anahim Lake. Pan needed no coaxing to go, waving goodbye to Ed Adams and Willie, who decided to stay and do the chores.

The word soon spread to their friends, that Pan was in town for his birthday party and the Holtes at Lessard Lake was the place. Before long there were three vehicles, jammed with people following them back north. One was a panel driven by D'arcy Christensen. Since the road wasn't that good, D'arcy's truck had to be towed with the Holte's tractor, until the final mile, when they came to the iced-over lake, but that only added to the fun. The other two pickups were able to make it through the tracks left by the sleigh and panel.

Pan reveled in the attention shown him. The table sagged under the weight of liquor bottles and food. And everyone became 'limbered up' as the liquor began to flow.

The celebration lasted into the early morning hours, in fact the revelers had come by daylight and they went home by daylight. During that time someone had fired a rifle, the bullets going through the ceiling; one woman had fallen through the floor into the cellar, when it broke as the dancing got vigorous; and fist fights, outside, settled several heated arguments. Pan and nineteen birthday toasters had went on a glorious toot. That time his reasonably sober image disintegrated. "Yer eyes look like two piss holes in a snowbank," Jimmy Holte told Pan as they left. Betty had taken a dim view of the whole proceedings. Their ride home, was a headache for Pan in more ways than one.

"Pan was a coniver," and if he poured a visitor a drink from his Royal Crown bottle, only he knew it was cheap booze that he had used to refill the bottle. Each little incident of tom-foolery he pulled off was an inner victory to him that he relished.

Ken (Willie) said, "Dad figured it took a better man to stay out of a fight than to get into one." And as far as we could find out, Pan only mixed it up with one man. Details are sketchy, but apparently on this one and only occasion, he saw a fellow that he figured had a licking coming, handed his jacket to a friend, walked across the street, faced the man then "stomped the hell outa him."

Pan wasn't much for 'grunt' work either, and usually could finaggle a way to get someone else to do the hard jobs saying, "He was so damned anxious to do it, I jist backed away and let him at it."

Betty said Pan was "afraid of anything with a handle on it," and few, if any, can attest to having ever seen him on the business end of rake, hoe, or 'muck stick.' Garden work, digging post holes, or shoveling manure wasn't Pan's forte and any time this sort of work arose, he was soon riding over the horizon on some errand, checking traps, checking water holes, looking for a stray, carrying a salt block to the cattle at Sill Meadow, or some other reasonably logical excuse that left the blister raising to others.

But, "Pan was a patient teacher," Gordon Wilson reminisced. "When I went to work for him on the ranch, at 15, I didn't know from scat, and Pan managed to make a competent 'hand' out of me."

Pan was as inventative person. As so often was the case, being isloated from town, when something would be needed around the ranch, he would put his mind to the problem and nearly always came up with a substitute item that would work.

Happy, who as a young man stayed on at the Home Ranch for several years, recalled one occasion, when Pan sold him a horse, after he had moved from the Home Ranch to his own place in Sleepy Hollow. Searching about his cabin where they had made the deal, Happy couldn't find any paper so Pan carefully tore off an empty beer bottle label, wrote out a bill of sale and unceremoniously, handed it to Happy, who has kept it as a momento to this day.

Another time, when Pan wanted to pay Happy for helping at haying, again no paper. Once more he used his ingenuity, he tore the flap off a beer bottle carton and made a cheque out on it. That Happy couldn't keep. When he took it to the bank to cash it the teller asked, "Whatinell's this?" Then after looking it over, muttered, "Mighta known it would be something Pan Phillips would dream up."

The old 'Riley Show' on television, in the 60s, could have been patterned after Pan. When Riley would say,

"Don't confuse me with facts, my head is set," it could have come straight from Pan. Once he made up his mind, right or wrong, it was "damned hard to change it."

He was outspoken, almost to a fault, and he never cut a corner in presenting his side on an issue, nor held back criticism when he felt it was due, yet he was respected for this very attribute.

But his word was his bond, good as gold right down to the last detail except with his family. Pan had a set pattern of treatment for them, another for the hired hands, and yet another for visitors. To him it was a lark to keep the family all guessing as to what his intentions really were; to keep the hands guessing what prank would be next; and to keep visitors enthralled with stories he had pre-judged they wanted to hear. His children and most everyone else, who visited the fishing camp later, stated they became reacquainted with Pan on a different plane.

Pan had one standard admonition for the kids that covered all occasions. To supress all mischief they were into or headed for and as a reminder of work to be done, he'd say "Quitcher fartin' around," which took care of them all.

Pan was a worrier about the economy, politics, and the world in general, even though in the Blackwater isolation, they seemed detached from the world. He had a habit of assuming the worst from any economic report he received and read a lot to sort out what bearing it had on his life. All his reading, though, wasn't of a serious nature.

Often he would sit in his rocker by the heater evenings, and read Betty's romance magazines which he had hidden from her, only giving them up after he had read them entirely or she found them first.

While reading, he enjoyed smoking his pipe. One evening he was automatically filling his pipe from the usual tobacco can, while keeping his eyes on the story he was reading as best he could. He tamped the tobacco, struck a match off the seat of his pants, then settled back puffing contentedly, sending smoke clouds above his head.

Suddenly, there was a close, loud bang. Pan's pipe blew apart, leaving him with a short piece of stem in his mouth. "Jesus Christ!" he yelled, startled, but not hurt. "Jesus Christ, what happened?" He stared up at part of the pipe bowl imbedded in the ceiling.

It didn't take too much detective work to figure out what had happened, because when he jumped up, a shattered 22 short casing fell to the floor from his lap. Willie was the accidental culprit, for he spent many hours playing with tobacco cans, Pan's full one included, and usually had some 22 shells in his pocket. Somehow a shell had fallen into the full can and Pan hadn't noticed it when refilling his pipe. From then on Willie parked his shells at the door when he came inside and Pan lent full attention to tamping the tobacco into his new pipe.

Pan was a very modest person. He would walk a quarter mile to get behind a bush to relieve himself. And as such, he expected modesty in his family, too. Once he "gave Betty hell" because she served tea to an Indian man while wearing shorts. Diana and Gayle often would get the word from their Dad too, for wearing scanty outfits.

Perhaps the most embarrassing moment in Pan's life happened at the Anahim Lake Stampede. He was standing by the arena talking with Alex Fraser and Dr. Holley, when a very old, Indian woman rode directly up to them on horseback. She pushed the horse's nose up against Pan's chest as he stepped back between his two friends. Pointing a finger right at Pan's hawk nose she told him, in a voice loud enough for everyone nearby to hear, "Pan Phillips, you'um damned horse thief!"

Without giving Pan a chance to respond, she swung her horse about and rode, haughtily, off into the crowd. He was speechless and red-faced from embarrassment, but not from anger. To the ex-Wyoming cowboy, being called a horse thief was the ultimate insult, and he felt low enough to "walk under a horse without his head touching the belly band." It was not clear exactly why or what brought the accusation out, but it was believed there was a misunderstanding over a colt Pan knew to be his and the Indian lady was sure it was hers. Pan had tried to settle the matter with her when he brought the horse in off the range, but was unsuccessful .

The cattleman's code was one Pan followed throughout his ranching days. It was that you never asked another man how many head of cattle he had, no more than you would ask him how much money he had in the bank.

Once when a greenhorn asked how big a herd he had, Pan replied, "When I'm feeding them in the winter, too many. When I ship them in the fall, there's not enough." And on another occasion he was heard to say, "More than ten and less than a thousand."

He was thought to have a high I.Q., a photographic memory and total recall on stories and incidents of all kinds. Although, it always took a bit of urging for him to relate this story.

In 1957 a friend from Eastern Canada was visiting the Home Ranch. They were out on a trail ride, camping at Kluskus, when a bright light came through the air, stopped, descended and hovered over them and the trees near where they had camped. It appeared to be an all glass flying machine, emitting a sound as if many small motors held it in the air. Then abruptly it "zinged" off towards Nazko at a tremendous speed, disappearing from sight in moments.

Another time, while bringing in cattle from the meadow to the Home Ranch corral, Ed Adams and he saw what looked like a giant bubble helicopter. It came down close enough where they could see it very plainly, hovered, then ascended straight up and was gone in seconds.

Pan, and both men, firmly believed they had seen space ships, but Pan was careful who he told about the U.F.O.s, "Don't want people thinking I'm 'tetched' in the head."

Pan's appearance, on the trail during the summer, matched the cowboy image most people's mind drew of him. However, it was not a matter of 'show' with him, what he had on at any given time was practical and functional. He could care less if they were western cut or not. He did wear a standard, cowboy styled, Stetson hat though. It kept the sun out of his eyes, the rain and pine needles from going down the back of his neck and in the winter he could wear a bandana under it, tied under his chin to protect his ears from the cold. When hooded parkas came out he made a change to them.

Chaps and a short slicker were necesary to protect him from the brush, limbs and rain, when herding cattle or horses. He added spurs to his boots only when necessary, depending upon the horse he was riding.

On his feet in the winter, Pan wore hand made, buckskin moccasins with heavy wool socks inside. Then he added Indian rubbers, which just covered the moccasin bottoms, to keep them clean and dry. Later when the artic 'pak boots' came on the market, he wore them using the widest stirrups he could find so the boots would not hang up in case he had to get off a horse quickly. Of course, during the warm months, he wore the standard western boot.

In later years, at the fishing camp, the Stetson gave way to baseball caps touting some product or another and usually a free gift from a customer. Pan's battered old Stetson came off the wall only occasionally, but was always a conversation piece. To this day (1985) it still hangs on the same nail on the fishing camp wall.

One time, we had an appointment with Pan, to meet him at Jess Ketchum's office in downtown Quesnel. Jess was then the manager of the Cariboo Tourist Association. We waited on the street for Pan, and waited, not seeing anyone coming towards us who resembled him. Then we recognized, sorta, the shuffling figure coming towards us, it was Pan. He was wearing a bright red cap, a blue windbreaker jacket, denims, and a pair of romeo slippers.

"For Christ sakes! What'er you dressed like that for?" we said in unison. "Jess wanted to meet the true Pan Phillips, cowboy of the Blackwater, and here you're not even wearing boots."

"Jest camouflaging myself. Gettin' tired of tourists stopping me, askin fer an autograph, like I was somebody important."

In all honesty, we don't know if he was sincere or not. We had felt during our association with Pan that he relished the attention most of the time. Others that we interviewed agreed, but maybe there were times when it became a nuisance for him.

We uncovered only one account of Pan ever wearing a suit and tie and that was at Ken's (Willie) and Andrea's wedding, June 10, 1971. No one can recall ever seeing the suit before, or after, so we can only assume it was borrowed or rented. A suit and tie man, Pan was not.

Pan's friends and neighbours liked him for himself and as Lizzie Paley said, "We were always happy when Pan stopped by our place. We talked about the country and ranching mostly."

He worried about his friends, Whites, Indians, Americans, Europeans, all--when they had troubles, cabin fever, or feared something, Pan would talk them through their anxieties and get them to take a second look at the situation. He was a good sounding board and they appreciated his advice.

Too, he was concerned about not only staying on a friendly basis with his neighbours, but worried about them as people. From Tsacha Lake, around the mountain to Anahim Lake, the population only numbered twenty some when Pan lived on the Home Ranch. With that limited number of people, a close bond was built between them all. Losing anyone to the grim reaper was indeed soul rending.

Many of the people he became close to, after his arrival in the country, were his seniors by quite a few years. Thus it was inevitable that as time marched on, he should be faced with their loss. In several cases it could be no worse than losing a close family member, and Pan mourned them all. He was particularly upset when he got word that his original partner, Rich Hobson, had died and that Toby Cave, flying out to pick him up for the funeral in Vanderhoof, had to turn back because of bad weather. Although they had gone their seperate ways many years before, Pan still felt very close to Hobson. He was very sad that he didn't get to pay his last respects.

Again, when his brother, Fred, was killed in a highway accident in New Mexico, by the time the word trickled through to Pan the funeral was long since over. Pan really grieved, for Fred and he had become reacquainted through his visits with Fred at his Arizona home and they had become close, as brothers should be.

In a somber moment, Pan told Betty, "I ain't in no rush, but I hope I go before any more of my friends, or family, pass away. There's too much hurt each time."

"You had to stand back and watch Pan to learn his personality. He had many sides."

—— Bunch Trudeau

BLACK CATS AND LADDERS

"Hell, I'm not superstitious, Jist don't want to take chances," Pan told Happy Thompson, but we just can't buy that. From what we learned, and personally knew about him,he was about as superstitious as anyone could be. We could write a couple chapters to prove our point, but instead we will run a few 'for instances' by you, to give you an idea just how superstitious Pan really was.

On a cold winter day, Pan was preparing for a freight trip to Anahim Lake. He had a four horse team hitched to the sleigh with plenty of hay aboard to feed the horses on the way in and cache for the return trip, plus his sleeping bag and other necessities.

With everything for the trip done, he walked into the house for a last warm up and a cup of coffee. By chance he glanced at the calendar which had been crossed off day by day. It was Friday, the 13th.

Without another word Pan went outside, unhitched the horses, covered the hay, and removed his gear from the sleigh, then returning to the house he shucked his heavy clothes, lowered himself into his favourite rocker and called it a day. He wasn't about to start a trip on Friday the 13th.

Pan was born on Sunday, March 13, 1910, and somwhere along the line, he had confused that Sunday date with Friday. He always said it was bad enough to be born on Friday the 13th, let alone go out and ask for trouble on that date, too.

He once told Alfred Bryant, "I was born on Friday the 13th, married on Friday the 13th and I figure I"ll die on Friday the 13th!" He was wrong on two counts for sure. He died on Saturday, May 28, 1983. We were not able to confirm that he married one of his three wives on a Friday, so he may have been mistaken on that score too.

On one occasion, Alfred Bryant was at his Talleywacker Ranch and knew Pan was due along most any day on his way home with a load of supplies. However, after noting the day on the calendar to be Friday and the 13th, he allowed that he wouldn't see Pan that day. But around midnight he was aroused by the distant sound of trace chains and creaky harness. A horse's whinney alerted him that he hadn't been dreaming. He jumped out of bed, put on his clothes, and went outside with a lantern, in time to see Pan rein his team through the front gate. His eyebrows were covered with ice, the sap was running from his nose and he looked half frozen. Before Alfred could say anything, Pan's first words were, "Didn't remember until a few miles down the trail what day it is. Shoulda turned back. The trail was fulla downed timber, and I've spent hours chopping."

Another day, Pan and Happy were out hunting. While riding along Pan got to fingering the shells in his coat pocket. Finally, he took them out and counted them. He had thirteen. He shoved them back, then had a mental fight with himself, his frugal nature pitted against his superstitous nature, finally taking out one shell and tossing it away. That left him twelve.

When they arrived back at the house, the first thing Pan did after removing his gloves, was to blow on his hands to warm them and then pull out the makin's to roll a cigarette. With the cigarette in his mouth, he searched his pockets for the lighter. He couldn't find it. He emptied his pockets on the kitchen table and re-counted them.

"Jesus Christ, I musta threw away my last bullet lighter instead of a shell," he admitted, sheepishly, to Happy and Betty.

"That'll teach you to be so damned superstitious," retorted Betty.

Pan would never knowingly start a project on Friday the 13th. Family and friends tried to bait him many times into doing something, but to no avail. Yet there was the one time he had no choice. We, (the authors) had known Pan for many years, and had arranged through our advertising agency, to round up a bunch of dudes for a trail ride through the Blackwater along the MacKenzie trail to Pan's fishing camp then south through the Home Ranch, over the mountains on Pan trail to Anahim Lake. A fifteen day ride in all.

Response to the advertising, in the States and Canada, was excellent and soon a group of outdoor lovers had committed themselves for the trip. They were coming from New Jersey, Ontario, Montana, California and points in between. They were secretaries, bankers, loggers, scientists; some of whom had never been on a horse.

We had set a firm date to meet Pan and Rich Boland, our partners in the enterprise at Tietown, a Blackwater crossing N.W. of Nazko. By the time we had reached Pan, through correspondence via Anahim Lake, and the message hour from Quesnel radio to give him the date, Rich and he had no choice but to leave the fishing camp on Friday the 13th.

In midst of our preparations we received a message from Pan, carried from the camp via a phone call from a flyer-fisherman returning home to the States. "Pan wants you to change the date set to meet you people at Tietown. "Make it a day later."

"Bullshit! No way. Can't do it, the date for our people to leave Quesnel is all set."

"Just telling you what Pan wants."

"How come?"

"He doesn't want to leave camp tommorow, on count of the day being Friday the 13th. If you keep your time schedule, he'll have to. You've got time to call the radio station with your answer for the evening messages."

"I don't think they would relay the answer I'd like to send. Anyway thanks for calling us. Buy you a drink for the phone call sometime."

The next thing we did, was call the radio station and asked to have a message sent to Pan Phillips and Rich Boland in the Blackwater.

"What would you like to say?" the girl inquired politely.

"Bull shit! No way! Signed Jack and Darlene Brown."

"I'm sorry, but we can't put that on the air."

"Okay, send this then. No way. Have to keep same date. People arriving Quesnel from all over hell."

"We can't say 'hell' either."

"Okay, strike the 'hell' and get the message on the evening program for us, please."

By late Sunday afternoon, we had rounded up all the would-be-cowboys and cowgirls at the airport, and had them in a bus headed for Tietown. Along the way, we picked up Rich, who had ridden out to act as a guide for the bus driver, with a companion, who had a taken his horse back.

"How come all this crap about changing dates?" was the first thing we asked him.

"You know Pan and his superstitions - he didn't want to leave last Friday because of the date, but we had to, to be in time for meeting you today." Rich grinned.

When we got to the river crossing, transferred our supplies, by wagon to the other side, there was Pan. Horses, wagons, tack, young Mary Alexis, who would be Darlene's assistant camp cook, the Harrington's, and several others, were there to see us off. As usual, Pan was the center of attention, gimping around on a home-made crutch.

"What the hell happened to you?" we asked.

"Horse kicked me. Knew damned well if we started out on Friday the 13th, somethin' bad would happen."

Later that day, it was discovered that the pinto mare Pan had brought out for Darlene to ride, had shoved a stick up its groin and was going lame."Jist no sense in tempting fate." Pan snorted. And if we heard that once in the next fifteen days, we heard it a dozen times.

Down the trail, when he had had time to think it out, he may have doubted the wisdom of his words, for that particular trail ride turned out to be one of Pan's most profitable ventures, plus giving the fishing camp an undeterminable amount of publicity.

The dudes loved the ride and spread word about Pan Phillips, and little wonder, for all Pan did on the entire trip was take advantage of his sore leg, by sitting by the fire, spinning yarns, or on the seat of the chuck wagon thinking up pranks.

Knowing what we do now about Pan Phillips, we would most certainly have inspected that 'sore leg' to be sure a horse really kicked him and he wasn't just shying away from camp work. Seriously - it was a great trip, Pan enjoyed himself to the utmost and so did the rest of us. Being on the trail with him for fifeteen days was an experience we will never forget.

As a final word, as to our assumption that Pan was superstitious,consider the fact that he would not walk under a ladder. And if a black cat crossed his path, he would find any excuse to let the trail get cold before proceeding. We rest our case.

"When Pan suggested you do something a certain way, you had to really think twice about it, cause it might well end up a joke on you."

————Alfred Bryant

A CHUCKLE BREAK

Tales of Pan's jokes along the trail are legend, too. Few are the men, and woman, that have ridden with him, who have not felt the blacklash of a limb across their face; been thrown from their horse because of a pine cone steathily slipped under their horse's tail; a burr shoved under their saddle blanket; or conned into crossing a stream at the deepest spot; or in some other way fallen prey to the master prankster.

Many of those pranks were carried out without the thought of the consequences, but there is no record of anyone getting more than a few bruises or anyone getting really mad, for Pan's "Hee hee" and joking remarks usually tempered their ire.

At this point we will deviate from the normal dictates of writing a biography and give you a laugh break, a solid chapter on some of Pan's more famous pranks, and a couple pulled on him in return.

In the early days, before Shorty came riding into the Home Ranch, thoughts of the feminine gender stacked up like cordwood in the lonely men's minds. It didn't take a second invitation for Pan and Rich to stop work and go visiting when the occasion called for it.

It had been a long dry spell for them, no booze, no dancing or funnin for quite a while when via the moccasin telegraph they got word that there were two eligble young ladies staying at Cyrus Bryant's ranch. That was all it took. They laid aside their tools, and allowed as how they needed a few days off, were on the trail early the next morning.

Pan was wearing his regular cowboy duds although he had rinsed out his pants the night before and dried them by the fire. Rich was decked out in his finest. He even sported a white shirt and tie that he had dug out of his duffle bag. Now that was just too much of a good opportunity for Pan to pass by and he thought on it as they rode along. Rich was lagging a fair bit behind, as Pan's horse could outwalk the critter Hobson was astride.

Finally, a plan hit Pan. Watching carefully, he eventually rode up on a bog made to order. Right through the middle were tracks, obviously made by some long legged moose calf Pan figured. He skirted the bog and was just on the far side, his horse standing where the tracks exited, when Rich rode out into the clearing up to the bog's edge.

"It's okay. Come on across," Pan yelled, and beckoned.

Rich, who should have known his partner by then, rode right into the mire following the tracks. His horse, sinking, began to spook and then fight, throwing muck and water high into the air as it tried to gain solid ground. By the time the pair reached Pan, Hobson's neat white shirt was covered with mud and the rest of his clothes a disaster.

"Jesus Christ. How come yer goin' in to visit in them dirty duds?" asked Pan straightfaced.

Rich had been had again - his reported reply is unprintable.

On one of Pan and Alfred's freighting trips, it just happened to be the big July 1st, Dominion Day celebration, in Quesnel. Naturally they had to take it all in. With a few shots under their belts, they were really enjoying themselves like a couple of sailors on leave. They came upon an old gypsy woman as she came out of her fortune telling tent, closed the flap, then hastened down the street probably to lunch. Here was a ready made opportunity for some fun Pan wasn't going to miss. He pulled the tent flap aside, inspected the contents and found that, sure enough, the old crone had left her robe and head shawl on the chair and her 'crystal ball on the table. He immediately opened the tent telling Alfred to hawk up some business. Alfred, always ready for a good joke, fell into the spirit of things and began his idea of a gypsy chant while Pan got the robe and shawl on, hiding his shirt and head with just the tip of his nose exposed. The table hid his jeans and boots.

"Cross the fortune teller's palm with silver. The gypsy will tell everything you want to know. Only four-bits for your past, present and future. Come in, come in! The gypsy sees all-knows-all-and tells all!"

Luck was with them. Just about the first possible victim-ah, prospect that came along was their friend Dude Lavington. Alfred pressured him into the tent, "for the good of the cause."

Dude sat down at the table rather reluctantly, across from the 'gypsy' and plunked down his four bits to have his fortune told. The 'gypsy's hands crossed the crystal ball and there was some mumbling being uttered.

Finally, words came that were as clear as a bell, "Yer past, present, and future doesn't amount to a shit," was the prediction.

"Damn you, Pan Phillips. That big nose shoulda tipped me off when I walked in here."

Dude was another in a long list that swallowed the bait.

Bunch Trudeau tells of the time Pan rode into the Bryant's ranch at Corkscrew Creek, ran into the house and told Jane Bryant that there was a very sick Indian man at an Ilgacho native party, down at the Dean River. "Musta drunk some poisoned hooch, 'er somethin."

Everyone turned to Jane in time of illnesses, she being a nurse. She was not one to hesitate when it came to treating the sick, white man or Indian. Outside it was 30 below zero and dark. Jane donned her heavy clothes, grabbed a lantern, went out to the corral, caught and saddled her horse then returned to the house to gather her medical supplies, putting them into the saddle bags. She took an additional minute for one last cup of coffee.

Pan couldn't contain himself and began to "Hee hee," giving himself away. When Jane realized Pan had duped her, she let him know that she was pretty disgusted. From then on Pan shied away from playing any jokes on her.

The hired ranch hands were open game for Pan's pranks and he seemed to sleep better if he had something to think over and chuckle about that had happened that day. Shag Thompson had joined Pan's crew as a young man and Pan respected and liked him, but Shag learned early that if he asked a question to mull over Pan's answer in his mind to decide if it was a straight answer, or if Pan was pulling his leg.

Somewhere in their conversations, the subject of a shotgun pellet pattern came up and Pan told Shag he'd show him soon as Betty's wood was in. Shag hustled off to the wood pile and the stage was set for Pan; he busied himself while Shag shagged wood. When done, Pan took a shotgun, and walked to the creek bank,

choosing a spot where the water was wide and slow
moving. The rest of the crew stood back to watch, sensing
that Pan was up to something, as Shag came to join them.

"Now, tell you what, Shag, you take this shotgun, aim it
right into that calm spot in the creek, then look real careful
where each shot hits. That's called the pattern. You kin tell
by it if you'd hit a duck, or anything else you were shooting
at. Go ahead and fire away now, but be sure and aim for that
calm spot jist this side of the eddy."

Shag took careful aim, fired and not a ripple appeared
on the water.

"Jesus Christ! You missed the whole damned creek!"
Pan yelled.

A look of disbelief spread on Shag's face; wide grins,
hidden by their hands, showed up on the audience's faces.
But Pan, unable to keep his straight face, began "Hee hee"-
ing which tipped off Shag that somehow he had been taken
in. Pan had carefully removed the shot from the shell in the
gun, while Shag chopped wood.

Another young lad* working for the summer at the
ranch, was eager to learn and posed many questions to
Pan. Somehow the subject of gold in the country came up,
the young man asking Pan if he had ever seen any in the
Blackwater, and more particularly in the creek nearby.

"Hell, yes! replied Pan. "Seen plenty of colour right
here in the yard."

"You have?"

"Sure. Ya go get that gold pan outta the tool shed and a
shovel. I'll show ya where to dig."

When he got back within minutes, Pan pointed out the
first place to dig. "Try'er right here. Dig a hole down about
three feet or until you hit gravel. Then call me. I'll come out,
take some gravel to the creek, pan it out for ya and tell you
if yer on the right track."

In a short while, the lad appeared in the house, sweat
pouring off his face. "Got the hole down at least three feet,
to the gravel. Come take a look, Pan."

---

* Actual identity unknown. The story was repeatedly told us, each person with a different idea who the lad was. We believe it factual otherwise.

Pan climbed out of his rocker and went out to the hole. He took a shovel full of gravel from the bottom, sauntered to the creek, swished the pan in the water a few times without any instructions to the boy then tossed the contents back into the water, saying, "Yep, you had colour all right. Looks to me like it's lying to the east. I'll show you where to dig next." There was an exact performance after which Pan announced, "By golly, I think yer on to something here. That veins getting bigger all the time."

"Next time let me see that there black sand and colour before you throw it back into the creek."

"Okay, now here's where I think you should dig next."

There was no recollection of just how long it was before the lad woke up to the fact that Pan had him breaking ground for fence post holes around the ranch yard.

Gordon Wilson went to work for Pan at a tender, gullible age. Part of his wages were to be the training he would get in ranching. For starters Pan taught him how to drive a team pulling a wagon. Then with haying coming on, he advanced Gordon to driving a team hitched to the mower, but it was his first lesson that he will long remember.

Pan led off with one team and mower, Gordon having been instructed to lay a second swath right alongside Pan's first one. All went well until they got to one section of land covered with reed canary grass that had grown higher than a horse's back. To Gordon, it didn't look like a place to be taking the mower, but Pan yelled back, "Keep following me like you've been doing," as the mower bounced over unseen hummocks.

Gordon wondered what Pan was doing when he saw him stretching his neck, eyeing the grass ahead and making very slight changes in direction on the cut. But Pan had told him to follow, so he did until he saw the team sidestep to solid ground while the mower and he sunk in a bog. Gordon stuck to the mower like he was glued to the seat and came out the other side, wet and muddy.

Pan called back, "Pretty rough, eh kid? Hee-hee-hee." It was only then that Gordon knew he had been deliberately suckered into the mire.

It had been a long hot day on the trail and Pan had had little opportunity to spice up his life in any manner. Had he missed any chances for a prank, he wondered?

The cattle were milling about the feeding meadow; the wranglers were busy unhitching teams and unsaddling horses; and others were setting up the night's camp. In general all were glad the day's ride was over. However, it was still a long time until dark and there was some banter as how to spend the evening. Inspiration hit Pan and he rummaged around under the chuck wagon seat for his newest and most prized possession. A big, black box camera that he hadn't had a chance to really use yet. "I think we oughta get a picture of the last Chilcotin hanging and let's see - we'll need a victim. Ah - lessee, you'll do Happy. Come on over here, we'll do this Wyoming style and use the wagon tongue ."

Alfred agreed that this was one helluva an idea, but Happy wasn't so sure about it all.

Pan and Alfred got to setting the scene. The wagon tongue was propped up vertically, and braced from the ground with a sturdy limb. Next they strung a rope from the top end of the tongue and a hangman's noose was fashioned. Happy stood on a block of wood while another rope was attached to a cinch around his middle and hidden under the rain coat that they slapped on him. This rope was then taken up the collar and tied behind the hangman's rope, out of sight. The whole idea being that when the block was kicked out from under Happy, the cinch and rope would hold him up, yet a few feet away it would look as though there was only one rope and he was hanging by the neck.

"Jesus, that's great," Pan stated as he stood back to take in the final scene through the camera viewfinder. "Kick that block from under him, Alfred, and let's get the picture. No! Wait! Better jist ease the block out from under him. Don't want that safety rope slipping none from a sudden pull."

So Alfred gently removed the block and Happy began to play the part. Pan attempted to get the proper perspective through the camera lens meantime admonishing Happy. "Stop wiggling like that. Can't get the picture until you're still. There, that's better. Hold it now.

Lookee there, Al, he's even turning his toes in and bugging out his eyes, jist like a real hanging. Yer doin' great, Happy. Just a couple more shots and we'll take you down. Hee hee, sure gonna make a picture to show folks around here. Maybe we can get it printed in the papers. Okay, that does it let him down now Al."

"Jesus Christ, Pan, I think this cinch line has slipped. Help me get him down quick!" Alfred yelled. Pan dropped the camera and came on the run.

"Holly shit! We've really hung him! As Pan looked at the safety belt, there was little doubt that it had slipped and all the faces Happy had made, plus the turned in toes, had been for real.

Alfred started slapping Happy's face, meantime asking, "What'll we tell the mounties?"

"Hell, we'll just have to tell them it was an accident." Pan pushed on Happy's chest.

In a few moments, Happy stirred and opened his eyes. "Hey, he's alive!" A cheer went up and relief was evident on everyone's faces. One of Pan Phillip's pranks had almost backfired on him. Happy, to this day, cannot stand a tie around his neck.

Alf Iegler and Pan became friends when Alf worked in Stan Dowling's Anahim Lake store, where Pan traded. Usually Pan and Alf had ample time to swap yarns and tid bits of news, but on one occasion when Alf lived in a nearby cabin, Pan stopped by after the store was closed. He had had a few good belts and was feeling chipper, joshin' Alf more than usual. The weather was bitter cold, and Alf was complaining about it, so Pan had an instant suggestion. Why not take his old tomcat to bed with him, shove the cat down to the bottom of the covers and keep his feet nice and warm? It didn't sound like such a bad idea to Alf so he thought he would give it a go if he could get the cat to co-operate.

With this thought imparted, Pan said his goodbye and went out through the lean-to shed. A short time later Alf went into the shed intent on catching the cat, the thoughts of warm feet that night filling his head. The dim glow from his kerosene lamp shone through the open door and he spotted the cat in the shadows. He picked it up, talking gently, and went back through the cabin door. By the time, he kicked the door shut and walked to his bed, he began to realize that something was amiss. The cat didn't feel just right. A quick inspection told the tale, he'd been the brunt of one of Pan's antics.

On the way through Alf's shed, Pan had also discovered the cat. He had also discovered a can of paint, taken it from the shelf, found a brush, then liberally painted the cat. Alf didn't notice the difference in the cat's colour in the dim light. Nor was he able to get all the paint off his nightshirt. The cat lost most of its fur, but survived the episode. And Pan was still chuckling about it half way around the mountain, visualizing the results of his chicanery.

Even the children weren't immune from Pan's pranks. One year, Mary and Lisa Cassam rode over to the Home Ranch to spend Christmas with Diana, the girls all being near the same age. With not a lot to do in the snowed-in house, they began to badger Pan to take them for a sleigh ride. Came Christmas Eve and the weather warmed up a bit. Pan capitulated, but not wanting the bother to harness a team, he hitched up the hay sleigh to his tracked tractor, threw on some hay for the girls to set in, then picked up the squealing, giggling girls.

Pan put the tractor in gear and gave it gas. As they sped out into the meadow, he glanced back and saw the girls starting to hunker down in the hay. The tracks were picking up snow and throwing it back over the sleigh covering everything, including the girls in the sleigh bed. Pan "Hee hee"-ed and picked up speed. This threw the snow even harder and the girls began to yell for him to stop, but he pretended not to hear. The tractor, Pan, the sleigh with the screaming girls - all made a complete circle of the big meadow and then back into the yard.

When he stopped, three 'snowgirls' rolled off the sleigh, completely covered with snow from head to toe. Pan thought it was hilarious, but the girls thought differently - on Christmas Eve the girls sleigh ride had been a perfect set up for Pan.

The yearly cattle drive was over. The cattle were all in the corrals at Quesnel and the party at the Log Cabin Court on the west side of the river, was in full swing. Invited and uninvited guests poured in the door, each arrival depositing a bottle on the table.

"Doc Holley and Pan were trying to catch up on a year's gossip when Heinz Osmers, the worried motel operator, stepped in the door. Suspecting that Heinz had not stopped by to socialize, but more likely to try and put a damper on the party, Pan immediately asked him if he would have a drink first and palaver later, to which Heinz agreed.

Pan set out three glasses, one for Heinz, Doc and himself, then picked up the water pitcher and began pouring water in the glasses. He had water in two, when unseen, he flipped the bottle top across the floor. "Hand me that top, will ya, Heinz?" he asked the still belligerent motel owner. As the man stooped to pick up the top, Pan quickly grabbed a vodka bottle and poured it into the third glass until the vodka filled the glass evenly with the two containing water, making all three glasses look exactly alike.

As Heinz stood up and put the bottle top on the table, Pan asked, "How much rye you want with your water, Doc?"

"Just pour and I'll tell you when."

So Pan poured and Doc yelled "When," just as the liquid began to cascade over the top of the glass. It was one man-sized drink.

"I'll take the same," Pan said as he poured. "How much rye you want, Heinz?"

Since his background was one that honour would never allow him to be outdone by a bunch of cowpokes, and their friends, he replied, "The same."

"Well, here's to you. This is where we seperate the men from the boys. Bottoms up." Pan raised his glass to chug-a-lug the contents. Doc Holley followed suit and Heinz, not to be outdone, raised his glass while Pan and Doc watched with glee. If ever a man almost had his shorts knocked off by a drink, it was Heinz, but he managed to get it all down without choking and headed for the door.

"He won't be back to bother us any more tonight," said Pan. He was right, and the party went on and on until well after sun-up.

The following episode comes first hand, from co-author Darlene Brown

"The trail ride from Tietown to Anahim Lake had just left on its first day out. One of the major obstacles was the crossing of the Blackwater river in a particular wide, deep

"QUIET, DAMN IT. The message hour is coming on", was a shout that few that knew Pan, and been around him for any length of time, had not heard. During lunch stop, on the trail ride from Nazko across the Ilgachuz to Anahim Lake, Pan is shown listening to the messages while co-author, Darlene Brown prepares lunch. Bill Solowoniuk, wrangler; Mary Alexis, camp helper; and Jack Brown look on. Pan never did find out who lost the chair along the trail that Brown's sitting on, and he added that to his list of little mysteries that he loved to dwell on.

spot. The pinto mare that Pan had brought along for me, was limping, so I had jumped on the chuck wagon at the back end, sitting on a case of canned milk. My horse was tied on behind."

"At the river's edge, Pan had stopped to let a couple of the skittish female dudes also, get on the loaded wagon, then pulled down the bank, easing into the water. I knew Pan well, but had forgotten momentarily, his yen for pranks."

"Midstream, Pan stopped the team and yelled over the noise of the water, "we've jist got too much load for these horses. Someone will have to get off.Not giving his remark a second thought, and since I was one of the trail ride hands, I obeyed the command without question."

"My boots had hardly hit the river bed when Pan broke out "Hee hee"-ing. I knew at once that I had been another one of his victims. The water was cold, and I was waist deep in it, but I had no choice except to hop back onto the wagon, red-faced, then listen to Pan's chuckling the rest of the day. Everyone had a good laugh at my expense."

Pan so loved a joke that he is probably the only man known to have tried to pull a prank on a pair of less than loving grizzly bears.

He was riding his horse along a ridge one day, when he happened to look over the edge, down into the creek. There two young grizzlies were pawing for spawners in the water. He couldn't resist the temptation.

Tieing his horse to a nearby tree, he crept up to the edge of the high bank and began pelting one of the bears with rocks, it then looked over at its companion and cuffed it across the head. Pan thought this a great joke, so he heaved a fair sized rock at the other bear, who did the same thing reached over and cuffed the first one across its head. By this time, Pan couldn't keep still any longer and let go a "Hee hee." If two rocks created so much fun Pan wondered what a handfull would do. Just then, however, Gin, Pan's faithful pooch, came running out of the woods, where he had been scouting for squirrels, looked over the bank and started barking at the bears. The bears looked up, saw Pan and the dog, and immediately charged up the bank. Pan ran for his horse. It had already smelled and heard the bears grunting up the slope so was raring to go. The race was on.

With the two grizzlies in hot pursuit, Pan raced along the ridge. Upon glancing back he could hardly believe what he saw; the bears were closing the gap between them and his horse. Gin, running alongside the horse, had been taught to heel an animal on command, so Pan figured if ever the dog was going to earn its keep, now was the time. He directed the dog to the bear's heels. Both grizzlies slid to a stop , turned to get at the dog while Pan rode into the clear soon to have Gin catch up none the worse for wear.

Another prank that backfired on Pan, and later he admitted to friends that for the first time in his life he had known real fear, for if his horse had slipped and fallen he would have been hash 'Ala Phillips,' on the grizzlies' menu.

Not too many men can lay claim to having gotten back at Pan for the jokes he had pulled, but for one of them, Alan Styvascent, got even. Pan had one prank he liked to play on any unsupecting person and got away with it a few times. He would get to a river ahead of his trail companion, cross where it was shallow, then ride along the bank to a deep spot. He would then back his horse to the river's edge and watch over his shoulder for the other rider to appear.When he emerged into sight, Pan would spur his horse, appearing to be just climbing the opposite bank and the rider would urge his horse in the water, thinking Pan had just crossed there and it was okay.

Alan and he were on the trail and Pan decided to have some fun by pulling his river stunt on the fairly inexperienced city dude. Alan came trotting along quite a ways behind him, saw Pan on the opposite bank and didn't hesitate, but spurred his horse right into the river. The horse sunk nearly out of sight and so did Alan. The horse came up swimming hard, but there was no sign of Alan surfacing.

Pan jumped from his horse, one worried man. "Jesus Christ! Jesus Christ!" was all he could say as he paced the river bank.

What Pan didn't know about Alan was that he was an excellent swimmer. He had automatically drawn in a lung full of fresh air when he realized he was going under, then had swam underwater, coming up under willow bushes down stream. From that vantage point, he watched Pan frantically running up and down the bank. But finally he relented and gave Pan a hollar. Pan's face flushed deep red and his chin began to quiver, a sure sign that he was boiling mad. His joke had backfired, but he wasn't as good a sport as he expected his victims to be. His hours of silence the rest of the day told Alan that he had really got Pan's goat.

No one could take credit for getting back at Pan in this manner, yet one incident gave cowboys, ranchers and the natives, in the Blackwater the biggest laugh at his expense that they ever had.

It was on one of the annual fall beef drives, during a

pitch black night. The wolves were howling,the wind was blowing and the cattle were restless. George Aitkens was riding night herd until they bedded down. He was already mounted and making his first circle when he noticed a figure coming out of the main tent, holding a lantern and walking over by the trees, obviously to relieve himself before hitting the sack. George, famous for his clowning around and obscene remarks, yelled at the long-john clad figure.

It was Pan, and George's yell startled him. He swung his head to look in that direction just as a gust of wind came across the meadow, then hit the trees in sort of a minature whirlwind. The lantern swung in his hand. There was the sizzle of burning flesh and Pan's scream of anguish brought the whole camp to life. George spurred his horse to go see what happened. Pan was jumping up and down, holding 'the family jewels' in his hands and cussing up a storm. He'd been had by an act of God.

"All the hands had a different idea on how to treat a singed pecker," related George, but Pan suffered many weeks after.

What worried Pan the most was that there was no way to silence his companions and he was positive soon the whole country would know of his plight.

Late one night at the fishing camp, when all the guests had turned in, Pan doused the lights in the lodge and headed for his bunk. Outside he walked over to his three wheeler, started it up and gave it the gas. It didn't move. After several tries he shut it off and walked the short distance.

Next morning, he went out to try to figure out what was wrong with his machine and found that it was tied up short to the picnic table leg, which was set into the ground. Someone had played a small joke on him, but he had to take a lot of ribbing about it from the fishermen.

Pan's pranks, or jokes, even carried through from beyond the grave.

After his death, Rob, and Pan's grandson Jon, were in the fishing camp lodge putting Pan's personal things away. Looking for a snack, they simultaneously spotted two small boxes of raisins.Each with a box, they then sat down, their tastebuds already anticipating the tasty moursels. But when opened, they found the boxes were full of small moose turds.

"The best thing that ever happened to this country was
the invention of chain saws and mosquito repellant."
——Pan Phillips

RANCH LIFE

The radio played an important part in keeping Pan,
Betty, the children and hired hands sane during the winter
months. Pan would work out the schedule on what they all
wanted to hear in the evenings, or what he thought they
should listen to. Pan didn't like 'soaps.' "Gunsmoke," "Lux
Radio Theatre," "Johnny Dollar," "Art Linkletter," and
"Dragnet" were their favourites. If any one of them were
late coming in from chores, or a ride, they would "Darn
near kill their horse," to get back in time so as not to miss
the programs.

The radio batteries were one of Pan's main worries.
They were the standard large flat batteries of the day, and
Pan knew almost to the hour how long each one would
produce enough 'juice' to keep the radio playing. If all the
batteries went dead, there went their entertainment, so
Pan had several set rules on the radio use. They did,
however, have a wind-up phonograph which provided
music in the off hours.

During the trapping season, Pan would sit, evenings, in
his rocker with a beaver, or marten, spread out on a board
across his lap, skinning it out while he listened to the
radio. Bigger animals he laid on a bench in front of him to
work on. Willie got the job of carcass disposal.

In the winter Pan would be excited as the kids when
the second snowfall hit (the first cleanses the air) for it was
time to make snow ice cream. He would lay out a table oil
cloth to catch the fresh snow and keep it clean. Then when
there was an accumulation of a few inches, Betty, or Diana,
would carefully scrape up the clean white flakes into a
large bowl. Betty would then add cream, sugar, and vanilla,
beating it smooth with a big wooden spoon. The result was
a soft ice mix that parallels today's soft mix served in the
fast food outlets. Pan could literally eat a half gallon at a
sitting.

Eaton's catalogue provided them later, with a hand
cranked, wooden ice cream maker and they then had 'real'
ice cream whenever they had a milk cow.

TRAPPING WAS A MAJOR PART OF RANCH LIFE in the winter. Pan is shown standing in front of the Home Ranch house holding a fox skin. Coyote "Prairie wolf" hides hanging in the background, meant money in his pocket and food on the table to Pan.

Running out of supplies in the dead of winter, was an occurence that the Phillips family tried to avoid, but it did happen. One time it was tobacco. Everyone, but the kids, smoked and they were all in the throes of a nicotine fit after all the butts had been salvaged and smoked. All, but Pan were making the most of it and he decided to create some smoking material. Seasoned cow manure, mixed with moss and burdock seeds were put in the oven to dry, mashed up, then Pan lit up. "Not too bad. Hell some of that stuff they sell in stores now days is nothing but barn sweepin's anyway," he told the rest, not understanding why they didn't want to give it a try. "No not bad atall," he added while puffing deeply on the highly aromatic mixture.

There were a few times, even though they thought they had planned their supply list well, that they ran out of kerosene for the lamps, forcing Pan to make several 'bitch lights.' He would take an empty tobacco can, cut it almost completely around about one and one half inches from the bottom, leaving a strip an inch wide from the top to the bottom. Then he would bend the strip over the top of what remained, cut a slit in it, ansert a strip of cloth for a dip rag, fill the bottom with moose tallow, then light the rag. It was certainly a poor substitute for a regular lantern, but it did throw enough light to get by with the cooking and chores. There was one big drawback to the light though, it stunk so badly that it had to be put outside when not in use.

As it was on many ranches, whether they needed it or not, once a week Betty would heat water for the family baths done in a wash tub by the kitchen range. Any of the crew, who figured their hide was getting too encrusted would borrow the tub, take it to the bunkhouse, heat their own water and scrub up in privacy. However, Rich Boland seemed to fear that it might "warp his hide" and it took considerable persuasion to get him near the soap and water.

"But, Betty, I jist had a bath last week, Sure don't need another this quick," he would plead.

"The hell you don't. I can smell you clear over here - now git!" Pan would yell, in agreement. Eventually Rich would take the hint, but it was like hitting a mule between the eyeballs to get its attention.

Mail was a vital link to the outside and each letter was read and re-read, especially in the winter. But, like supplies, sometimes the weather prevented Pan from getting the mail from Anahim Lake. During one such time, a batch of mail was picked up in mid-October and then they never received another batch until March 18th, when Pan finally got in on another freight run just ahead of the break-up. He returned with eight mail sacks full - it was Christmas all over again.

To celebrate, Pan had slipped a bottle of CC into one of the bags and when it was discovered they had a drink. Then it was put back on the table, forgotten, while the mail got their undivided attention.

Willie was just a toddler, and he too was ignored as he climbed upon the table. The bottle caught his eye, so he tipped it up and took a swig. Betty and Pan were so engrossed that they didn't notice when he took a second swallow, or a third. Before long little Willie collapsed. One look at the bottle and they knew what had happened.

Betty was scared and Pan was excited. They tried everything they could think of to make him vomit, to no avail. Both were afraid the liquor would kill him. Betty never slept a wink that night. All the fun had gone out of the Christmas mail. Willie slept right through until three the next day, then woke up bright and cherry, seemingly alright. Pan and Betty both breathed a sigh of relief, but that was the last time they ever left an uncorked bottle around where Willie could get to it .

"Jesus Christ, if it's not one thing it's a dozen," was all Pan had to say.

Occasionally something would come up to break the regular routine. Sometimes pleasant - sometimes not.

In early March of 1963, Pan became ill, so word was sent out and the RCMP came in and flew him out to Quesnel, where he stayed until the first of April. After Doc Holley had turned him loose, Frank Burns flew him back, landing his ski equipped plane on Styvie Lake's icy surface. Frank, another passenger who was enroute to Anahim Lake and Pan tromped through the snow to the ranch house. Pan knew that Betty was planning on going back out with Frank for a visit in Quesnel, so while the others 'coffeed up' and got warm, he hitched his tracked tractor to a sleigh, threw on some hay for easier riding and was ready to take them back to the plane.

By the time Betty had all her things collected, the men were warmed up, Pan had the sleigh in front of the house and they all climbed in, kids included. At the lake Pan steered out onto the ice, towards the plane. All went well until about a hundred yards from shore, the ice began to roll like waves in front of the tractor. It got so obvious that Pan's passengers started yelling and hollaring for him to head for shore, but for some unknown reason he stopped and shut off the engine. As he stepped off the machine, the ice began to crack, creak and groan. One of the men quickly unhitched the sleigh and with everyone's help, got it back

on shore. Pan made a run for it too, when he realized the ice
was actually breaking up. He turned back just as the ice
gave completely and his pride and joy, the tractor,
disappeared under the broken ice, sinking out of sight into
ten feet of water. It was one of those 'sometimes not'
breaks, and Pan worried until spring about how he was
going to retrieve the needed tractor.

The salvage job began in May, after the ice was gone.
Frank flew in mechanics, Warren Kerr and Willie Martin to
help. With the help of a grapling hook, pulleys and a team,
they got a line on the tractor and finally towed it backwards
out of the lake. The oil was drained; carbureator cleaned;
gas tank rinsed out and the gas lines blown; and the
distributor cleaned and dried. At the end of the fifth day,
the tractor started and was able to make it back to the yard
under its own power.

For awhile, the tractor episode gave them something
else to think about and talk about. As Pan told them, "Hell,
if it wasn't for bad luck, we wouldn't have no luck a'tall."

In the fall of 1966 mother nature gave them another
topic of conversation, except for Pan who wasn't saying
much after ending up with a lot of work. Pan, Betty, Diana,
Rob, Lloyd Bennett and Eddy Lifton, two extra cowboys,
hired for the drive, had all left the ranch on the fall cattle
drive. Rich Boland got the ranch sitting job. With his
chores done early one day, and being an avid reader* he
settled into Pan's rocker to read a "Duster" (western
story), getting engrossed immediately. The house was
warm and quiet - he had no forewarning of what was to
come, which was the worst wind to ever hit that area before
or since (1985).

Rich really wasn't aware of the seriousness of the
blow, until he saw the cat (and he swears to this) being
blown by the window. The house's thick sod roof and log
walls, muffled the storm's noise. It had sneaked up on him,
not that there was anything much he could have done
about it. The wind blew over a 500 pound hay rack; wiped

---

* Diana told us that Rich often carried a book in his hip pocket and is the only man she
has ever seen, who would stand up in a wagon boot, so his legs absorbed the shock of
the bumps, and read while driving a team!

out miles of fences, tumbling them like dominoes; blew everything that was loose out of the yard into the meadow; and blocked all the trails with a multitude of uprooted jackpines. It took Pan and his entourage, ten full days to cut and hack their way back after the cattle auction. Upon their arrival, they found Richard surveying the damage.

All the crew had their work cut out for them, for months to come.

Visitors were joyously welcomed, but often put to work. Bunch Trudeau and Ann McKilvington, two close lady friends from Anahim Lake, rode into the Home Ranch to talk to Pan about driving some cattle to Quesnel with his herd. They had made the long ride in one day and arrived "pooped out" and sore. Both dismounted, their first port of call being the outhouse after "Howdys" had been exchanged. Pan waited patiently at the house. When the women walked in, he had a scowl on his face. "Fer Christ sakes, don't you two know bettern to walk by the wood pile without bringing an arm load in? Then, unable to keep a straight face, began "Hee hee-ing.

He was promptly told to "Go to hell," and they got on with their conversation regarding the cattle, while Ann cut Pan's hair. No one with tonsorial know-how got through the ranch without Pan persuading them into giving him a clipping. A hippie he wasn't.

Peter Alexis worked at the ranch every summer and would move his family with him. His job was repairing fences, cutting wood, helping with the haying, and then either taking care of the ranch while the fall cattle drive was on, or going with them as a wrangler. In reality, Peter was a vital part of the Home Ranch life, and Pan's closest native friend.

Facing grizzly bears was just a part of ranch life, too, and everyone connected with it, from the family to the ranch hands to the animals, all had their scares. Pan, himself, had been chased up trees; had outran them on horseback; and had been chased up on the cabin roof. He had had to kill them in the yard, by the back door, and in the meadows. They, plus the wolves, were the most disrupting factor in ranch life and the most destructive factor in raising cattle and horses. The bears came in all sizes and temperments. A few could be bluffed, but others either held their ground or charged.

One morning Pan got up, glanced out the kitchen window to see what kind of a day it was going to be, and almost looked eyeball to eyeball with a grizzly that was trying to paw some peelings loose from the grass. Pan hollared, thinking the bear would leave, but it didn't see him so it raised up on its hind legs to look around. Its head was even with the top of the clothes line post, one mighty huge bear. Pan got his gun off the wall, fired a shot, trying to scare it away rather than take the chance of wounding it. The shot worked, for the bear dropped on all fours and ran across the creek. When he was sure the animal was gone, he went outside, got a ladder and measured from the post top to the ground - it was just over twelve feet high, which meant the grizzly had to be record size.

In May, 1968, Pan received word that one of his long time friends in the Anahim Lake area, Connie King, had been badly mauled by a grizzly, but would recover from his injuries. This report brought the dangers facing him and his own family into focus. The theme of Pan's next lecture to them all was to keep a watchful eye out to avoid any encounters with the meanest and most unpredicatable of the species.

Most of the ranch equipment was limited to the horse drawn variety, however, there came a time, in the early 1950s, that Pan decided he needed a tractor. He bought an older model International Harvester, then nursed it in over the 100 mile trail from Nazko before the spring breakup. He had visions of all the time he would save, for to get a job done with the team, he first had to catch the 'jingle horse;' saddle it; find the team on the range; bring them back in; harness and hitch them to the rig - by then anywhere from one to two hours were lost.

Pan was right to a point, but what he had forgotten was that it takes gasoline, and a considerable amount, to feed a tractor, and that had to be freighted in too. So the tractor didn't get as much use as Pan had envisioned and the jingle horse and team never faded from the everyday working scene. In fact, the horses were such an intregal part of Pan's life by then that he would invaribly yell "Whoa" to the tractor, when he wanted to stop, then

TOO CLOSE FOR COMFORT. Pan is shown with the grizzly he shot less than 100 yards from the Home Ranch kitchen, "Willie" (Ken) and Diana peer at the bear with childish curiosity, too little to realize the danger the beast had posed to the family.

remember the clutch and brake.

After the airstrip was in and it was a bit easier to get gas into the ranch, he bought a second tractor, an International 250 half track model for getting about better in the mud and snow. At first Pan absolutely refused to let anyone else drive either tractor. To his young son Willie, driving the machines were a childhood dream, but as much as he would beg, Pan stuck to his guns. Willie left the ranch before Pan eased up on his policy.

Other equipment included a big harrow, used in clearing brush, that had teeth almost like plows - curved and sharp; a buck rake that had wooden teeth; a couple of mowers; and a little log skid 'go devil' which served to haul smaller one horse loads around the ranch yard. Pan's original Bennett buggy was sold to George Aitken, when he struck out on his own. Pan then proudly bought a new Massey Harris rubber tired wagon and drove it out from Quesnel.

Pan never left a sharp axe at the woodpile, or carried one on his trips, for which he was chided many times. He was convinced that a dull axe could split wood better than a sharp one, and when his word was doubted, he would take a sharp axe to the wood pile to prove his theory. Continually, the dull axe would split the blocks, while the sharp one bit deeply, sticking without forcing the wood apart. Pan made a believer out of many.

The makings of a sawmill was freighted in by Pan and over the years it cut many a board feet of lumber for not only his needs, but even for Indian homes on government contract. The kids commandered a goodly quantity for such use as tree houses, etc. Pan never complained about them using the lumber to build with, "Gives 'em somethin' to do besides cutting up harnesses and getting into other trouble." The harness reference pertained to Willie, who had decided to try a brand new knife out by cutting what he thought was an old trace. Making this remark to someone while in Willie's presence was Pan's way of reminding him, that although he may have been forgiven, the incident had not been forgotten.

Before mosquito repellent became readily available on the market, the pesky insects could, and did, make life miserable everywhere in the Blackwater. It was ideal breeding ground for them, the country covered with bogs and marshes, flooded during high water, then lying stagnant most of the summer. Not until the heavy frosts came, did the mosquitos die off. On the trails, people covered as much of their exposed skin as possible, without roasting from the heat, then were constantly batting them away from their faces. The animals tried to swish the swarms from their backs with their tails, but could not do much to get them out of their eyes, ears, and noses - except by constantly rubbing their legs, or a nearby tree, with their heads.

Large smudge fires were built around the trail camps in late evening and kept going through the night. The horses were tied as close as possible, but it was usually a losing battle against over-whelming numbers.

Betty's sister, Margarite, from Gibson B.C., sent word one spring that she would be visiting them, giving them the time she would arrive in Anahim Lake. Pan sent Happy, along with Betty, to drive the team, (not that Betty couldn't) and help her with camp chores. The timing of her visit was wrong, for it was in the worst part of the mosquito season. They were just about eaten alive both ways. On their one night stop enroute home, the smudge fires just didn't seem to do any good, and they arrived at the ranch with big welts on their faces, necks , and hands, their eyes and ears swollen. Later, when Pan took Margarite back to Anahim Lake, it was just as miserable.

Riding home from the stampede one year, they headed over the mountain following the 'Pan Trail,' also dubbed 'Tobacco Road' due to a few special trips made by Pan when he was about to run out of the 'makings.' The first stop out of Anahim Lake was at Corkscrew basin where they immediately built a large, smokey jackpine fire. Betty had a sizeable, wide bottomed pan that was ideal for heating water quickly and it was put on the fire promptly for heated tea water. Pan sauntered over to take a look, then barked at Betty, "Get them damned mosquitos skimmed off the water. Don't mind them in my stew, but can't stand them in my tea." The mosquito swarms were flying into the smoke and hot air above the fire, getting their wings singed and then dropping into the heating water, covering is as fast as Betty skimmed them off.

Some individuals, especially the natives, seemed to become immune to the bites, but Pan never did. He hated mosquito season with a passion.

Burning off old meadow grass and weeds was a way to give the new grass a chance to grow earlier in the spring and it gave the land a good shot of pot ash, which aided nature's growth. Pan had his own ideas about this and the Forest Service had their ideas. Needless to say, they didn't see eye to eye. The Forest Service looked on the meadow fires, particularly on leased Crown Land, as a definite fire hazard and woe be to those that they caught in the act of setting one ablaze. Their fears were based on the fact that the fire could get into the deep spruce and jackpine needles, smolder for weeks, then break out into a major forest fire. The same held true for peat moss.

On one calm day, which Pan figured was just right for a fire to 'accidentally' get started in the lower meadow, he set out on Old Whitey, a box of wooden matches in his pocket. Once in the meadow, as he rode along, he scratched one match, then another, lighting them with his fingernail so when they dropped into the tinder dry grass, it flared up instantly.

The fire was just as he had planned by the time he was half way around the meadow perimeter. It was then that he heard an aircraft engine in the distance. He spurred Whitey towards cover under the jackpines, hiding as he watched the plane circle overhead, then disappear. Pan "Hee hee"-ed to himself figuring he hadn't been spotted and watched as the fire began to eat its way through the tough old grass.

But the next time he happened to be in the Forest Service offices, he got a message, maybe more of a lecture. The head honcho told him in no uncertain terms that if he did not want to be seen the next time he wanted one of those meadows to 'accidentlly' catch fire, he had better not ride a white horse.

As any young girl might, Diana kept a diary and like all diaries the contents are privy only to those who have written them. However, Diana extracted the following excerpts for us to include here, which enlightened us as to the ranch's monthly chores. They varied little from year to year.

January: Can be cold and generally a snow month. Usually rustled cattle (moved them about to let them find feed through the snow) until New Years, then started feeding them hay. Not a month for too much activity except checking the horses in Sill Meadow and Sleepy Hollow.

February: Warmer. Some thaws. Dad did some freighting. Started cutting lumber logs or fence rails. Hauled hay from Sill Meadow (three miles east of the ranch), If there came a thaw and the moon was right dehorned calves. (The Farmer's Almanac guided Pan in many of his activities.)

March: Often windy and spring storms. Freighted from Anahim Lake. Still hauled hay from Sill Meadow. Checked horses. Brought in any animal that was thin to be hand fed.

Spring birds arrived. Moved the cows in close to buildings as they usually started calving about March 20th. Someone took the graveyard shift, another took over at five a.m. Wasn't uncommon to have a sick or cold calf in the house.

April:Still busy calving. Some colts would be born. Sheep would be lambing. Checked horses. Burned meadows. Would be fairly nice, but still getting snow. Sawed lumber.

May:Turned cattle out. Watched new calves and colts. Burned range. Rode and fixed fences. Got in firewood. Brought in horses and trimmed their feet. Turned them out into summer range. Around the 20th spaded and planted the garden. Broke horses, sheared sheep.

June:Branded and turned cattle out. Built fences. Some hot weather. High water time, so flooded (irrigated) the fields.

July:Spring holiday. Spent 10 days going to the Anahim Lake Stampede and getting back. Hunted horses. Got teams ready for haying. Checked cattle. Cut firewood. Started haying at the end of the month. Grizzlies this time of year to watch out for.

August:Haying. Checked cattle. Fenced in stack yard (hay pens). Started gathering in the beef. Took out hunters, Broke more horses and shod them for the beef drive.

September:Finished haying. Fenced stack yards. Herded in the rest of the beef. Took out hunters. Broke horses, picked more for the drive and shod them.

October:Took cattle to Quesnel. (It usually took the whole month to drive the beef to town and get back to the ranch.)

November:Got remaining cattle in off range. Brought horses in too. Cut and sawed winter firewood.

December:Weaned calves and started feeding them. Checked cattle and horses. Did odd repair jobs.

To give you an additional idea of Pan and his family's ranch life just before and right after he sold the ranch, we have taken the following quotes from letters they, and Ed Adams, wrote to Rex Barlett.

From Ed's letters:

December 14, 1969 - "Pan is leaving the 15th with team and sleigh for Anahim Lake. Should be back before Christmas. Have been hunting horses for a week. Pan and Rob shot three deer last week."

April 18, 1970 - "Has been a long hard winter. Lost a lot of calves."

September 25, 1970 - "Pan and Richard busy with hunting. Had good luck with caribou and moose. Pan just came down from the mountain with four hunters. They got four caribou and four moose. Cattle drive leaves October 1st."

December 12, 1970 - "It was 38 degrees below and a foot of snow on November 28th. Had a hot dry summer, so we're short on hay."

December 5, 1971 - "We've got six inches of snow and it's now 18 below. Radio went dead. The cook left in November, never did come back. Me and Richard cut 260 logs on the Home Ranch (then owned and occupied by Bob Anthony) which we'll saw this winter and take down to Pan's new place (the fishing camp). Had a good crop of hay this summer."

April 30, 1972 - "Had a real nice winter. Snow up to a horse's nose. Stayed on all winter. Moose eating hay off the sleigh while I was loading it. Sandhill cranes and ducks have arrived, so spring can't be too far away. Didn't lose any stock this winter. Half the cows have calves now. Have had mail once since Christmas. Haven't been out in five years, but don't miss it at all."

December 18, 1972 - "Pan's been in town since the middle of November. Last summer me and Pan took wagons to Anahim Lake for freight. The school teacher makes home brew, one bottle and you can lick a buzz saw. When they have a party it lasts for a week. Pan had good luck with hunters. Lots of caribou, not so many moose. Too many wolves. Well, that's the way she goes."

From Betty and Pan's letters:

August 20, 1968;- "Haying was held up because of rain this year. We've got hunters coming August 29th for Pan and Richard. We all went to the stampede, had a real nice time. We had to get the predator hunters out to kill a grizzly that's been killing our cattle. Seems to have taken care of the problem. The cattle sale is October 18th, and November 3rd, but don't know which one we'll make due to the late haying."

November 19, 1968 - "Dropped to 15 below. Had a few inches of snow then it shot up to 50 degrees above."

February 6,1969 - "We didn't get our Christmas mail until Feb. 5th this year. Betty went into Quesnel to pick up Robbie and didn't get back, so the women spent Christmas in town and we spent it here at the ranch. Very cold weather, 46 below and Anahim Lake had 70 below a couple nights. Lasted right into February. Makes it hard to feed the stock."

March 23, 1969 - "Pan's leaving on the 22nd to go get Diana. She's been working out all winter. This will be his last trip out until after the spring breakup."

May 26, 1969 - "We're getting the garden in. Pan has gone up the creek to check on the cattle, and Ed's over at Tommy Meadow checking the yearlings."

June 21, 1969 - "Had to replant the garden because of the hot dry spell. A garden means so much back here where it's hard to get fresh vegetables. We've had rhubarb pie already."

August 8, 1969 - "We've got new neighbours moving in twenty miles from us. They have a plane and are keeping it on our airstrip until they get their own built."

September 28, 1969 - "The rain is slowing our haying. We've still got one batch in hay cocks. We'll leave on the cattle drive on October 4th. There will be four TV men along with us this time. Richard is going to stay home to care for the hunters. Robbie kept us supplied with meat this summer, fish and geese, too. Pan had four Oregon hunters the first part of September, got four caribou."

October 6, 1969 - "Pan and Richard just got in with hunters. Got three moose, four caribou and two deer. Pan's going into town with them to get something done to that leg of his."

February 1, 1970 - "Pan has gone into town for the mail. A friend dropped us some mail in mid-January. He had wheels on his plane so couldn't land. We didn't get everything."

February 16, 1970 - "We've just received our Christmas mail. Haven't had mail since the middle of December. The winter has been mild. Freezes a bit at night is all. Pan is heading into town again in a few days for freight. We're taking all the cows to Ed's (Sleepy Hollow) for feeding until spring."

December, 1972 - "Merry Christmas" signed 'Old Pan'. (Somehow we never thought of Pan as 'Old.' The word just didn't suit him.)

Pan had a hard time keeping his head above water as the ranch was far from being a money making venture. If it hadn't been for Ed Adams and Richard Boland working as hands for ten years, receiving only their room and board, he wouldn't have made it. Pan was acutely aware of this and realizing his indebtedness to these two men, he made every effort to show them his appreciation. However, when interviewed, neither of them felt Pan owed them a thing. Through his friendship with Pan, Ed, in essence found a second family. Richard not only found a second family, too, but ultimately received enough money from his share in the guiding business to outfit him and get started in logging on his own. So whether Pan realized it or not, he was in some way reimbursing the two for their help and friendship.

"When Dad (Pan) figured something needed doing, he put his mind to it, and it got done."
——Diana (Phillips) Rempel

BUILDING AN AIRSTRIP

Over the years, a few winter visitors had landed ski planes on the Home Ranch meadow. Pan hadn't given much thought to putting in an airstrip for full time use, but with the advent of better aircraft, and increased air travel, he began to take note of the planes flying over-head and gave the possibility of having his own strip considerable thought. Betty agreed with him, that it would be a valuable asset to the ranch.

Jed Campbell, from Quesnel, had walked a 'cat' into the area and had used it to punch in an airstrip for Tsacha Lake lodge owners. After it was completed, Pan inspected it carefully; there was no question in his mind but what he could put one in his big meadow a lot easier. So, in 1961, he laid out and staked the strip, then on September 20th, he went to work.

First Pan used a six horse team and heavy disc to cut up the sod along the proposed strip. Then he used a two horse team, pulling a scoop, to level off the high spots and transport the dirt to the low spots. Final leveling was done with a heavy log drag, pulled by a four horse team.

Pan judged that once a team and wagon, loaded with people, could run the strip's length without any of them bouncing off, it was good enough for airplanes to land. He did get in several trial runs.

The next year, after the ground had dried, he removed the white crosses he had placed at each end of the new strip, for they had indicated to the pilots that the airstrip was not yet open and useable. Once they were removed, the fly-in visitors started to arrive.

At first the many arrivals impeded the efficiency of the ranch operation, but later, as the fly-ins leveled off, it brought about a tremendous change in ranch life. Mail arrived almost weekly, brought in by any one of the flyers who planned to stop by for coffee or a meal. Since the strip was built a half mile northeast of the ranch house, it kept Pan busy running the tractor back and forth to get those who flew in. Sometimes, they came in flocks and Betty would just get the dishes washed from one bunch when another plane full would arrive, hungry.

"Maybe we oughta open a restaurant," Pan jokingly told Betty.

A good number, however, would thoughtfully bring something to add to the ranch larder.

During haying season visitors weren't exactly ignored, but they couldn't be given the attention that was given at other times of the year. Except when it came to young love.

Rich and Diana both were at an age that the opposite sex was an important part of their life, whether it was haying season or not. Rich had met a young lady in Quesnel, who was a pilot and owned her own plane. Diana, that same summer, had a young man courting her, who also was a pilot. Quite often the two flyers would land the same day, usually during mid-afternoon. Pan got especially vexed by their visits because once they landed, he could not expect any more work from Richard or Diana for the duration of their stay, which usually included supper. He had nothing against the two young people, but secretly wished they had found the 'loves of their lives' elsewhere. However, as the summer wore on, he learned to tolerate their company, remembering that he too, was young once.

Two years after completion, the airstrip was instrumental, in a sense, in bringing a great deal of sadness into Pan's and his family's life when thirty-one year old Len Cave was killed after he stalled his plane, a Piper PA—12, on final for a landing.

Len worked at the ranch as a hired hand, but before coming out he had earned his pilot's license and bought a plane. His flying experience was on the short side. He chose a day to fly into town for ranch supplies when the visibility was good, but there were strong gusty winds. There his brother, Toby, tried to get him to lay over until the weather improved and the wind subsided before he started back. Toby's plea fell on deaf ears, Len assured him he would have no trouble.

Upon his return, he flew over the house and Betty came out to wave at him. Pan was in the field repairing fences and stopped his work to watch the plane land. He saw the crash. Len was killed instantly. His death upset them all terribly. Pan had built a strong bond of friendship and respect with Len, so much so that he asked Len's family to bury the lad's ashes on a little knoll overlooking the airstrip and meadow, with the mountains in the background, one of the most beautiful spots on the ranch. Small jackpines were used to make a fence, the propellor off his plane was used as a headstone and Toby planted a small blue spruce at the grave site.

When Pan later sold the ranch, the tree died. He considered that a bad omen and often commented aloud that maybe he shouldn't have made the sale.

"Pan Phillips was the only man, I ever knew, who could
drive cattle over 150 miles and have them gain weight
on the trail."

—— Ed Adams

THE FAMOUS CATTLE DRIVES

More has been written about, and more romance
attached to, the cattle drives through the Blackwater
country from Anahim Lake and the Home Ranch, then
anything else in the history of that era. There have been
many longer drives, but none under more adverse
conditions, yet it held the title of North America's longest
cattle drive. For over thirty years, Pan Phillips, with the
help of his family and hired hands, pushed the herds over
200 miles (in later years, 125 miles) of torturous trail,
brush, mud, swamp and often, snow, to become a legend in
the eyes of the world.

Many people at various times joined the drive -
dudes, neighbours, photographers and even a CBC
television crew. Pan even talked us into making one of the
drives with Bob Anthony, after he bought the ranch from
Pan.

The excitement and the glamour of the drive broke
into full bloom when it hit town. When the drive was under
the auspices of the Frontier Cattle Co. and Pan was the
Home Ranch foreman, the whole town of Vanderhoof
would turn out to help herd the cattle into the holding
corrals. During the final days of the F.C.C., the drives all
terminated in Quesnel, which Pan continued. It was
strictly Pan's own enterprise then, aided and abetted by the
neighbours who threw in with him along the way. When the
cattle hit the holding pens at Quesnel there was not a
doubt about it; Pan Phillips was the hero of the day.

Perhaps Doc Holley tells it best. "When I was just a lad
in high school, I remember one of the most exciting things
in my young life, was to be at the bridge over the Fraser
which connected the west side of town to downtown
Quesnel when word spread that the cattle drive was
coming. As I stood alongside the road, shoulder to
shoulder with most of the town youngsters and oldsters,
no circus parade ever drew more appreciation than the

sight of the herd stringing out for a half mile or more to file across the bridge. Every eye would be on the whiskered, buckskin clad cowboys crossing with the cattle, their well worn chaps showing signs of constant brushing with dead limbs and brush, their coats bearing a rip or two, their Stetsons soiled and sweat stained. Truly each personified the image of a true western cowboy that people talked of, young ladies dreamed of, and young men, including me hoped to be. For many of us they were our idols."

Pan never led the procession, he usually brought up the drag. When someone spotted him, the cry "There he is!" would go through the crowd and Pan grinning from ear to ear, would proudly ride across the bridge.

It was a time to celebrate, and celebrate they did. Although Pan had a reputation to maintain as a two fisted drinker he never took on the 'joy juice' until the cattle had all been put in holding pens, watered and fed. Then he would schuck his chaps and heavy coat and settle down to serious drinking with his countless friends.

There is no doubt, that a complete book could be written about Pan's escapades on the cattle drives; about his family and neighbours; about his daughter Diana and his sons Ken(Willie) and Rob, who could ride and herd cattle as well as any man; about his wife, Betty, who drove the chuck wagon, made the camp, set the fire, packed water and did the cooking, plus tending to her own team. They were a part of Pan's life and his legacy, but this is not the type of book for those tales, so we will touch only on a few highlights to give you a closer look at the cattle drive on the trail with Pan.

The 1940 Cattle Drive: - In those early days the cattle drive was still something of a novelty and Pan had yet to settle on a regular route to the stock yards at Quesnel or Vanderhoof. That year he elected to go via Dude Lavington's ranch on upper Baker Lake, then move on and join Rich Hobson's drive from the Batnuni. Dude and he got along famously and the rest period extended into six days before the two got their B.S.ing sessions polished off to a standstill. The hands hated to see it end as they had enjoyed listening in, when not out minding the cattle which were then still Frontier Cattle Co. stock. Many years later, Dude retired from ranching and took up writing.

The 1943 Cattle Drive: - Alfred Bryant drove his cattle across the mountains over the Pan Trail, from Anahim Lake to the Home Ranch, to merge his herd with the F.C.C. stock. From there they traveled further down the trail, meeting the Batnuni herd where,then, Pan, Rich Hobson and Alfred spent most of the night around the campfire, each trying to out-yarn the other. When they finally got the cattle across the bridge at Quesnel and into the stock yards their job was far from over. Due to an extra large number of cows to be shipped from Quesnel that year, the water supply went kaput so water for their animals had to be hauled from the river which was no easy task.

Pan had a knack for taking things in stride and when the others grumbled he remarked, "Hell. Ain't that bad, little more exercise will do us good. Might slow up our drinking a mite, but we got nothing but time to make it up."

The water was hauled daily until the cattle were shipped and the reports we got indicate that it affected their partying time very little.

The 1944 Cattle Drive: - Pan was kept away from home longer than usual this year, for by the time they got into Quesnel he had received word that he could get a higher price, per head, in Vancouver. The decision was made to continue on and the whole herd from the Blackwater was loaded into cattle cars. Pan, Joe Spiers, Major Franklin and Alfred Bryant volunteered to ride the uncomfortable caboose, making sure the cattle were tended while on the long trip south and unloaded at the stockyards in Vancouver.

It was, of course, during the war and licquor was rationed. Pan didn't figure his ration, Joe's and Alfred's would last them the trip down and back so he began to work on Franklin, a teetotler, for his ration. Franklin eventually gave in and at the first stop where there was a liquor store, Pan and Alfred led the reluctant man to the door where he balked like a Missouri mule. "Nosiree, ain't gonna do it! At 55, I've never yet set foot in a liquor store and I'm just not about to do it now."

No amount of cajoling could get him to change his mind and Pan finally gave up. He trotted to the nearest fruit stand and began making selections, Franklin and Bryant tagging along. Alfred wasn't any happier with

Franklin than Pan was. Pan paid for the enormous load of fruit, then said to Franklin, "Hold out yer arms. The least you kin do is help pack this stuff back to the train." Pan began piling the man's arms full, topping off the load with a watermelon. Franklin staggered off towards the train with Pan and Alfred sauntering behind - empty handed. One way or another, Pan wasn't about to let Franklin get away with a complete win.

Pan knew that Joe Spiers had the reputation for having the biggest appetite of any man in the Blackwater. He was soon to find out how Joe earned the title. On the way to Van, Joe tied into the fruit like it was going out of style. Then at the first cafe they visited, in Vancouver, Pan watched in amazement as Joe devoured two dozen eggs and a stack of pancakes six inches high. Jesting, Pan suggested that Joe should try a dozen fried oysters, claiming the place was famous for them, even though he had never been through the door before.

Joe gave it some thought, burped loudly and allowed as how he might just do that. An astounded waitress took his order and when she served Joe, then watched him clean the platter, as if he hadn't eaten in months, she shook her head in disbelief. Pan sat open-mouthed, all he could say was, "Jesus Christ. Glad I don't have to pay his bill."

The 1946 Cattle Drive: - This was a drive of Pan's Home Ranch herd and Rich Hobson's cattle, after the Frontier Cattle Company had been disolved and each man was on his own. Pan had pushed his cattle through in record time. Gertie Williams, a neighbour of the Batnuni spread, approached Pan and Rich about adding her eighty head to their drive. She was welcomed, as was the custom.

At Bouchie Creek it was decided to lay over for a full day to rest the cattle and for the crew to scrub off mud and sweat before getting into town. The next morning's light brought the discovery that all eighty head of Gertie's had turned back towards their home pastures. It was a mad rush for saddles. Pan, in the lead, with several wranglers following, galloped after them, trying to catch the animals before they got too far down the back trail.

Quite some time later Pan came riding into camp, alone. Gertie met him, a worried look on her face, as he dismounted. "Didja find them Pan?"

"Hell, no," Pan replied, his expression dour. "And we can't waste any more time lookin' for 'em either. The boys are on the way back, too."

Gertie's face fell, as she could visualize herself backtracking to her place, and maybe, just maybe, getting her cattle to market later before the heavy snows came. It would be quite a blow to her pocketbook, so she sat down with a tin of coffee to think on it.

Fifteen minutes later she heard the clatter of hooves, the bellow of cows and the whoops of cowboys as they ran her string back into the meadow. "Damn you, Pan Phillips, you'll be the death of me yet!" Gertie laughed. She knew Pan had pulled a prank on her again.

The 1947 Cattle Drive: - This was the year that a new dimension was added to the ranching history of the area. The summer before Alfred Bryant and his rancher neighbours from the Anahim Lake area, had scouted a cattle trail northeast over the Itcha's towards Baker Creek, trying to find a short way to the Quesnel market for their beef. The Lavington brothers scouted the other end, meeting on the Baezaeko. Work on the new trail was completed, and the two drives met for the first time in 1947, near the Baezaeko Flats. The merging meant a giant herd had been melded from many smaller drives, and the residents of Quesnel were awed by seeing that many cattle on the hoof.

As usual, Pan was on the drag and once again received much attention from young and old alike. We can't really say our friend, Pan, was a 'ham' but from what we have been told he certainly glowed in the attention and admiration shown him.

The 1950 Cattle Drive: - Gordon Wilson was punching cattle for Pan and glad for the job, plus the break in ranch routine when time came for the fall drive. Moving the cattle went with a minumum of problems, but by the time they got to Quesnel, Gordon was quite tired of grouse, beans and macaroni.

At the cattle sale, Pan had bowed his neck because he didn't like the price they offered, so he called Williams Lake, got a better price, and had forty head of his prime beef trucked down the road. "Figured I'd wise up the buyers at Quesnel a mite." Which he must have done, for there is no record that he had to take his cattle further than Quesnel after that.

The 1952 Cattle Drive: - Arrangements had been made again, for the Bryant and Dorsey cattle to be brought over the mountains, only this time to the Home Ranch, where they merged with Pan's herd trailing out to Nazko. Art Lavington, since the Quesnel to Nazko road was improved, had started a hauling service so he got the contract to haul the beef from holding pens two miles from the general store into the stockyards which cut off 50 miles from the drive.

Dave Dorsey had worked for Pan for wages the previous year, but Pan and he had made an agreement this year whereby Dorsey would work on a partnership basis at $8.00 per head for the Anahim Lake cattle to be split up among the cowboys. The arrangemant suited everyone fine, and after a days rest from their four day drive over the Pan Trail, the cattle were bunched in with the Home Ranch stock and under Pan's capable directions hit the trail again.

Their first stop was Paul meadow. Dave arrived tired and hungry, as all young men seem to be most of the time. He grabbed a hunk of jerky out of the chuck wagon and looked around for a place to sit and relax, finding a tarp thrown over some equipment off the chuck wagon. As good a place as any he thought.

"Jesus Christ! Get yer ass off there! bellowed Pan. "Yer sittin' on my new Coleman camp stove."

Dave jumped up, but too late. The rivets of the stove's side had popped from his weight, splitting the stove wide open, bending the metal.

Pan didn't seem to carry a grudge, but all the way to Nazko, he kept reminding Dave to "Watch were you plant yer ass." However, by the time they reached Quesnel, he was saying it with a twinkle in his eye.

Once in town, Pan advanced Dave some spending money on his share of the earnings. They had to wait two days for the sale and each day took its toll on young (18 year old) Dave's pocketbook. By the time payoff day came, the lad had borrowed exactly $206.00 from Pan. When Pan handed him his tally slip, supposedly with his additional money, all he got was the piece of paper. His share came exactly to $206.00. Pan was good at figures and wasn't about to advance Dave more than he judged was earned.

The 1958 Cattle Drive: By this time, the road between Williams Lake and Anahim Lake (Highway 20), had been improved so much that Stan Dowling's trucks had taken over hauling that area's cattle to market, freeing the ranchers from the long drive over the mountains to join up with Pan's drive. He was now alone, but also, by this time, Pan had a routine in moving his beef that suited him.

The first day out of the Home Ranch, Pan would push the cattle on the longest day's drive, 16 miles to Paul Meadow. This would take the 'starch' out of the animals, settling them into trail plodders, with just an occasional 'knot head' making a break for the timber or back home. The riders, and the herd, were pooped when they settled in for the night, but Pan tried to hide his lack of energy by being the last to stoke the fire and roll up in his sleeping bag.

On the second morning, Pan would roust everyone out early to get underway for Antoine Baptiste's place. The Indian was one of Pan's close friends and he looked forward to their evening talks around the campfire. "That Pan Phillips, he talk all night. Get no sleep," Antoine once told us.

Meantime Diana, Willie and sometimes one of the cowboys, would creek fish for trout to be fried for breakfast the next morning.

The third day would see the herd milling about at Kluskus, after a short drive. Pan would count the animals here and note with pride that "they hadn't lost a critter and all seemed to be in good shape." There was lush valley grass, good water and a natural holding area. The cattle were content, so there was no need to assign anyone to be a night rider. Too, they checked their horses, repaired harness and shod them if necessary.

Pan would bring the herd across Lashaway Chantyman's crossing on the fourth day. There they would lay over, letting the cattle rest during the fifth day. Time was spent visiting with the Kluskus Indian friends and again catching up on any repairs. Pan enjoyed the bull sessions immensely, and since most natives are shy people,

THE HERD, milling around on the hillsides above Kluskus Lake, at the end of the third day of the drive. In lower photo note the grazing horses still saddled, but with loosened cinches, and in the background "Old Whitey" tethered to the fence, ready for instant action should a grizzly, or anything else, spook the herd.

not addicted to long disertations, Pan liked center stage, keeping up a continuous conversation.

Throughout the sixth day, the cattle were moved on to Round Lake. There was no decent meadow there so they were corraled and Pan's wisdom in letting the cattle feed an extra day at Chantymans, came to light.

Rocky Mountain was the seventh day's stopover point after another long distance drive. There the cattle were hard to hold because of the small meadow and sparse grass, putting his cattleman's instincts to the test. A night rider would be put on, if the herd was extremely restless, and often Pan put his own bedroll in the middle of the back trail. On one such night, he assigned Rich Boland that duty. It was quiet and peaceful, the cow bells and jingle horse bell lulling all to sleep. Suddenly, Rich stated, "Hoofbeats seemed to be drumming in my ears. They became louder and louder, then stopped. When I raised my head to look, there was one of the team, its front legs hobbled, and its hooves against the edge of my sleeping bag." It was, obiviously, headed back home. After the camp settled down, towards slumber once more, Rich was still shaking from his close call, but Pan, considered it had been a joke on him and as usual his "Hee hee"-ing could be heard in the crisp night air.

The herd reached Moffet Harris's Place on the eighth day, the cattle being put behind fences on the far side of the river. Camp was set up near Moffett's house, near the back trail. Usually, there wasn't any trouble encountered there, but on the 1971 drive, when Bob Anthony was the trail boss after buying out Pan, a grizzly spooked the animals. They broke through the fence, crossed the bridge, scattered camp and people in all directions, and trotted down the trail towards their home grazing.

On the ninth day, Pan would bring the herd down into the valley at Nazko and pasture them overnight. The next morning, the tenth day, the cattle would be moved to a loading chute and hauled into Quesnel by Lavington.

With the advent of trucking, the excitement in driving the cattle across the bridge in Quesnel to the cheers of the spectators was gone. It was a small part of his ranching that had come to an end in 1952, and Pan still missed it.

The 1968 Cattle Drive: - That year wet weather plagued Pan's life and he didn't get his crew into haying until early August. He had to send word for the predator hunters to come in, track down and kill a grizzly that was taking a heavy cattle toll, and he had booked a hunting party for August 29th, all of which put them on the trail later than usual.

Near Rocky Mountain, they ran into an early snowfall, making the drive colder and harder to push the cattle, but the beef were at the auction yards in time for the November 3rd sale. By the time, they wound up their yearly 'salabration,' loaded the wagons and were back on the trail home, the weather had turned warm. The snow and cold eased back into Indian summer.

The 1969 Cattle Drive: - This was the year the legend of Pan Phillips was to spread even further, for the CBC Television directors had come up with the idea of filmimg "North America's Longest Cattle Drive." They contacted Pan through letters and the radio message service, striking an agreement of horse and equipment rental that was necessary for the trip, plus setting a price on meals. Lodging would be under the most handy tree or tent, whatever was their choice.

The drive got off to a fair start, cameras grinding, the television men taping up the usual sore spots on their bums, and Betty turning out extra scrumptious camp grub. Daughters Diana and Gayle were along, as was Robbie, who, at 13, had been the target for a behind-the-shed lecture, by Pan, in which he had suggested the lad display his best behavior.

All went well until they got to Kluskus and began to set up camp. The cattle were milling in the valley while the crew and guests got their first cup of coffee. The horses stood resting nearby, 'ground-tied' with saddles intact, until the cattle were settled in. It was a picturesque, serene scene - made to order for a good film, but not for long. To Robbie it looked like a natural for some highjinks. And he had the means to cause them, for on the way past Tsacha Lake Lodge, someone possibly with a wicked sense of humour, had given him a package of fingerling firecrackers. He had hidden them in his jacket pocket waiting for the right time to light them.

Robbie sauntered behind the closest tree, lit the firecrackers and threw them back at the lounging, relaxing riders. You can probably guess the result. Not only did it scare people, it scared the horses and aroused the cattle.

All the horses bolted - except the jingle horse that someone managed to grab, and with that jittery animal, Pan went to look for the rest. Bear in mind, the horses still carried saddles, had reins dragging, bore rifles in scabbards, and had slickers tied behind their saddles. It took two days to find them. By then, the cowboys, family and television crew had driven the cattle by foot to the next camp, thinking the horses might have gone that way. As it turned out, they had gone to the top of Poplar Mountain and when they came down for water near camp, the cowboys grabbed them. All saddles, scabbards, rifles and tie-ons were secure, only one saddle blanket had been lost. The show was back on the road except for retrieving the wagons from Kluskus, which was done that evening.

Meantime, Pan was so busy getting the drive on schedule, he hadn't allowed himself the pleasure of having a few words with Robbie, who suffered in anticipation of the eventual dressing down he expected from his father. But, Pan fooled his son. Once the matter was resolved, the horses back in camp and no major losses, Pan's temper had cooled, thus his words for Robbie were not what the boy expected. Robbie doesn't recall the exact words of Pan's lecture behind some scrub brush, but he said, "Dad wasn't mean about it and let me off with a verbal reprimand, although he did confiscate the remaining firecrackers."

The television film crew's efforts were well received and as a result there was a half hour long documentary aired on CBC's national network.

Quesnel in general, and the Log Cabin Court in particualr, were the scenes of a great celebration after the cattle had been sold. The Paley boy's often supplied the music and often it was nearly drowned out by the loud voices and laughter of all the people crowded into one big room. This particular time, Dave Dorsey was dancing with a young lass who had a decidedly English accent. His dancing left much to be desired, but he was attracted to the girl and it seemed the logical way to get acquainted. While they moved around the crowded floor, Dave kept her at arms length, very proper like. Pan stood by eyeing the two and when they worked their way around the floor near him, he couldn't resist. He lit a firecracker and dropped it at their feet. When it went off, the sweet young thing almost jumped on Dave's shoulders, she was so startled. Seeing Pan, a sly grin and emitting his usual "Hee hee" she made a quick comeback that took even Pan by suprise, saying in her clipped English accent, "Oh, Dave. I thought that was your heart that went bang."

Young Dave was speechless, and later Pan kidded him about letting the perfect opportunity slip by. "Ya coulda kissed her,er something, without jist standin' there with yer face hangin' out."

At the end of a particularly cold, cattle drive, Pan had been partying for the better part of a week and ended up at Doc Holley's place at Dragon Lake. Doc took one look at him and decided what Pan needed was to sweat the booze out in the sauna, so Holley cranked it up to full heat, got Pan into it and let him soak. When Pan came out he said, "Ya know, Doc, that's the first time I've been warm since I left the ranch two and a half weeks ago."

Pan was, also, having stomach trouble. The booze hadn't helped that any either, so the day he was to start back home, Doc Holley gave him a big dose of white coloured anti-acid medicine. Before he got to Nazko, Pan lit a cigarette and it made him so sick he laid off the smokes. At Nazko, he again lit his tailor made, with the same result. So he swore off smoking and managed to do without rolling his own for a full six months. By the next time he saw the doctor again, he was back puffing away, but related his experience. "It was either the steam bath or the white stuff that got to me and it ruined my smoking pleasure. Now that I'm over it, I kin smoke again without getting sick. One of the few comforts in my life is a cigarette."

Happy Thompson spent many of his Home Ranch years helping to prepare for the annual cattle drive. One time, Pan and he were moving cattle from one corral, cutting animals that were to be taken to market. Pan decided he needed to change horses, so instructed Happy to bring Trooper in from the meadow. Happy dismounted, grabbed a rope and started walking out. Half way there, he stopped to wonder where his brains were, he should have ridden his own horse out, then led Trooper in. What the hell? He decided he would ride the horse in bareback. He untied Trooper and with just the picket rope in his hand, swung aboard, riding in towards Pan. As the horse neared Pan, he whipped off his hat and started yelling, "Whoa! Whoa! at the top of his lungs.

Trooper always was a horse easily spooked so you don't have to guess what happened. Trooper stiffened his legs, humped his back and Happy went flying.

When he got his wind back, he blurted out, "What the hell did you do that for? You wanta get me killed?"

"It's a damned good thing I waved my hat and yelled whoa, or I don't know what woulda happened. I could tell that horse was getting ready to dump ya." Pan rode off "Hee hee"-ing.

Rex Bartlett and his wife Katherine, happened to be going through Quesnel, when one of the cattle auctions was on and met Pan there. They decided to go to the sale with him, sitting together, facing the auctioneer. Pan slipped away, Katherine noted a bit later, and assumed he had left to make a nature call, but about the time the hazers ran one of the mangiest looking old steers in the lot by the auctioneer, she noticed Pan behind him. Then as the man went into his final chant, Pan waved and without thinking Katherine waved back. "Sold!" yelled the auctioneer. Katherine nearly collapsed for he was pointing his gavel straight at her. Having been privy to the whole episode, the people sitting around her all broke into laughter, which made her even more embarrassed, thinking what in the world would she do with the old critter.

However, she lucked out, as the auctioneer noting Pan standing behind him "Hee hee"-ing, caught on and allowed that he would let them run the steer through again. Katherine had been another victim.

"Excitement seemed to follow Pan, where-ever he
went, what-ever he did."

——Steve Dorsey

BATTLING THE HORSELESS CARRIAGE

Pan Phillips went through life with an aversion to
driving a car or truck. He was far more comfortable behind
a team, on a wagon, or astride a horse. "There's somethin'
sort of peaceful about riding along, looking at the scenery,
slow like, so you can see somethin' even if it's only an
occasional glance up the bore of a horse's ass." Pan once
told us.

Which brings to mind a joke that he told around the
camp fire one night. Pan asked a dude if he knew what the
height of imagination was and the answer was "no."

"That's sitting on a cake of ice, letting someone blow
horse shit in your face, and imagining you're sleigh riding,"
Pan said, laughing.

When Pan arrived in Anahim Lake after the long trek
from Wyoming in the old Model A he found that only Stan
Dowling and the RCMP had vehicles in that area. Team and
wagon, or horseback, were the main means of
transportation. This suited Pan to a 'T'. He didn't cotton to
mechanized transportation anyway. But there came a time
when he realized that he should have a car. It would save
valuable time in traveling where there were roads, so he
bought an English Ford Prefect and left it in Anahim Lake.
He took a lot of joshing over his choice of a car as everyone
accused him of buying the cheapest thing on wheels, in
price and gas mileage. They may well have been right.

It was a sight to see, Pan driving, his hands frozen to
the wheel and his eyes glued on the road. One look and you
knew he was as uncomfortable as a rooster on a nest. As
well, since he was so used to the speed of a team, it felt to
him like he was flying when he exceeded 25 miles per hour.
The result was that he was the slowest driver ever to take
the wheel

Pan, Betty, Willie and Diana took a Stateside tour in
the Prefect, to Wyoming and on into Illinois to see Pan's
family, in the early 1950s. With Pan at the wheel, the speed
never seemed to exceed a fast walk and Betty swears a
couple of Model T Fords roared by them.

Pan believed in being legal, he did have a driver's license, but it hadn't come easy. On a trip into Quesnel with the car via the 205 mile gravel road to Williams Lake, he decided he had better 'legalfy hisself." He duly reported to the RCMP, produced his old worn out, illegible Wyoming driver's license to prove that he could drive and expected to be issued a B.C. license without ado. Such was not the case, for he had to take a driving test. This information brought out a bit of a sweat on his upper lip. He had heard that the examiner in Quesnel was "one tough son-of-a-bitch." But he was determined, after all he had driven the damned car from Anahim Lake to Quesnel so that ought to prove something he thought.

The test turned out to be a comedy of errors. Trying to follow the examiner's instructions, Pan breezed right through the first stop sign and got bawled out for that. On the first right turn, he didn't signal and got bawled out for that. When the examiner finally got him on a back street, he was instructed to back up for a block. The Prefect was all over both sides of the road and Pan got bawled out for that.

"Jesus Christ," Pan said. "I ain't figgern on driving this thing backwards around the country."

His final instructions were to "Park here," which he did. Very skillfully, too, Pan thought.

"What's that there?" the examiner asked, pointing.

"Looks like a damned fire hydrant to me. What's it look like to you?" It was, and he had parked right beside it and got bawled out for that. So it was back to the hotel room for another day studying the driver's manual. On his second test, he just squeaked by, but Pan didn't advertise this fact. It just sort of got nosed around on the moccasin telegraph.

Later when Alfred Bryant, after he had just got his license, asked Pan how he'd made out, Pan made light of it by saying, "If the old bugger hadn't been half boozed up, you'da never got your license." He was a great one for transferring any sort of embarrassment from the embarrassee to the embarassor.

Pan went visiting one day in the car, to the Bryants, and they had really hooted it up as he came in , driving, instead of astride a horse.

When he got ready to leave, Alfred and his crew walked out to the car with him. Pan climbed in, and started the engine while still chatting with Alfred, who stood by his window. Pan was so engrossed in the conversation that he failed to note the disappearance of the others. With a final "so long," he put the car in gear and hit the gas. The engine roared. The car failed to move. "What the hell," muttered Pan under his breath.

Unbeknowingst to him, the men had sneaked around behind the car and were holding the back wheels just off the ground. They let it drop just as Pan gunned the motor once more. The tires dug in, the car leaped ahead, and Pan damned near snapped his neck. For once it was Pan who had been tricked.

Pan was pretty proud of his automobile, and rented an old building for a garage in Anahim Lake to keep it in, while he was out at the ranch. Came a time when the local residents were planning to throw a dance, when someone suggested the garage as a place to hold it - the same one in which Pan kept his car. There was plenty of room, but it was decided a little more room wouldn't hurt anything, so a few huskier men picked up the front end and pushed the Prefect up against the wall until it was resting on the back bumper. A couple large boards nailed to the floor kept it in place. Time marched on - a couple months later, Pan came to town, put his team out to pasture, deciding to make a trip in his car. He opened the garage doors, finding he was on the other end of the stick, for the one thing the revelers had deliberately forgotten to do, was to take his car down from the wall. It still sat upended on the back bumper.

There were many periods when things were pretty lean, cash-wise, around the ranch. On one such occasion, Pan rode into town and traded the Prefect for an old, blue Studebaker pickup and 'boot money' for supplies. Then on a similar occasion, he sold the Studebaker. "Wasn't usin' them much anyhow," he told Betty.

When Diana hit him up for a loan to buy a year old, red, Ford pickup, in 1969, he was still without a vehicle, but didn't hesitate. The deal made being that she could repay him by making up the cattle count for the fall beef drive from her herd, which ultimately cost her only three scrub yearlings. In the meantime, the Ford pickup was parked in Anahim Lake, so when Pan went to town, he always found some reason why Diana had to go too.

As a result, Pan would want to go visiting this ranch, or that one and since he had loaned her the money to buy the pickup, he certainly expected her to play chauffeur, of which Diana took a dim view, having errands and visiting of her own in mind.

"Hell, you can drive this damned truck," she told her Dad. "It's got an automatic transmission. All you do is give it the gas and steer."

So Pan allowed he would give it a try, and found it wasn't all that bad, so while Diana visited friends, Pan would do his running around. At first he barely crept down the roads, but as his expertise in the truck increased so did his speed. One afternoon Diana was waiting in front of Baxter's cafe for Pan to pick her up, when she saw him turn the corner. This was long before blacktop, yet she swears she heard the tires screech. The truck came roaring towards her, at 60 per. Diana ran closer to the road and waved her arms wildly. Pan seemed to be enjoying driving if speed was any indication. However, as he sped by, oblivious to her, Diana saw that he had the same locked on, bulldog expression that he used to have when driving the Prefect; his eyes rivited straight ahead, and his knuckles white from the tight grip he had on the wheel.

"Where'n hell was you?" he asked her later.

When Betty moved to Quesnel after the Home Ranch sale, they bought a car, but Betty did all the driving as Pan never had the desire to renew his drivers license.

"Pan told me to make sure I gave a man a good hunt,
that was the ethical way."

——Gus Abel

HAPPY HUNTERS

Pan got into the guide-outfitting business a few years after the Frontier Cattle Co. folded and after his accident. Under his first license, he went to work for a man named, Lucas, at Trails End on Pelican Lake, still riding the side saddle and daring anyone to make a crack about it. He couldn't do the heavy work, but he soon became an excellent guide, having a knack for figuring out where the animals were feeding or bedding down. His wages were $35.00 per month, plus ammunition, tobacco and found. Times were tough and jobs hard to find. As far as we can determine, he guided for Lucas two years before joining in with Lester Dorsey. While Pan was out guiding, Betty and the hired hands took care of ranch chores.

We couldn't pin down the exact date either of when Lester and he entered into a partnership, whereby, they would book hunters out of the 3 Circle Ranch to pick up side money when things were slow at both ranches after haying season. But with Lester's wife, Mickey, handling the books, and his brother, who lived in Washington State, booking the hunters, their venture turned out to be a success.

At that time game animals were plentiful and the days of pampering hunters had yet to come. Their success rate was 100%, unless they happened to get a hunter who preferred to stay drunk, or couldn't hit the side of a barn. If a man didn't get his meat, or trophy, it wasn't the fault of Pan and Lester, for they continually led their hunters within sight of game.

The two men ran the guiding business for three years together and never changed their mode of operation. It was a rugged he-man hunt from the word go. The hunters had to have stamina, and a real yen for rugged outdoor living, as the 'out camps' were usually just a few shaggy, torn, old tents, around a big bonfire, with food cooked ala ashes and pine needles, flavored by an occasional dash of snoose from someone who's aim wasn't the best.

PAN WAS A SUCCESSFUL GUIDE, as indicated by this photo taken in 1949. He is on the left, in the plaid shirt, Steve Dorsey sits on the moose. The identity of the other two men remains unanswered.

Hunts were booked from the end of August through November, the later ones most often in snow and freezing weather. That was Pan's and Lester's own element, but for the average hunter, it was akin to a jackass running with a herd of bangtails. Lester's son Dave declared, "If the hunter wasn't a mountain man when he started, after ramming around in the hills for ten days with those two, he sure ended up being one - that is - if he managed not to get sick, busted up or frozen."

Toilet paper was never included in the pack lists. Most old timers agreed that, "If there's one thing that'll bring a man back to basics, it's wiping his ass with a hand full of marsh grass or wet moss."

Everyone was well fed, there were lots of potatoes, which would be cooked even though frozen, plus rice and dried foods that were light in weight to pack. Most certainly, it was far from gourmet food, but they had plenty. Added to the fare were grouse ('spruce hens'), and the traditional liver and onions, after the first kill.

You would normally think once word of this primitive operation spread, the results would have been that customers might be hard to come by, but such was not the case. Tales of ten days with the two roughnecks, were told around the plush country clubs in the States, so each year they had an ample supply of green horns. Some were even repeats. Fortunately, for Pan and Lester, it worked out that way, for neither of them gave any thought to pampering their clients to keep the money rolling in. "To those two characters, money wasn't nearly as important as getting into the bush, living with nature and having some fun, usually at the expense of the hunters," Dave added.

Pan's insatiable yen for practical jokes could have cost them customers, except, with his personality he could get away with a prank, where other men might fail miserably. One of his favourite camp tricks, was to get his own horse saddled up quickly, then set a near empty 'white' gas can near the fire, swing aboard and ride out of range to wait for the inevitable explosion. Horses reared and bucked. Men cursed, but many times only after they caught their breath from landing hard on the ground. Pan, settling his mount with a word or two, sat and watched the melee he created, "Hee hee"-ing as some unlucky soul hit the dirt.

Lester didn't cotton to Pan's jokes, he'd give him hell, but Pan kept on snickering, knowing that his friend's temper would cool down soon.

Game animals were prevelant in their guiding area. The guides never interceded with a hunter making a kill, unless a wounded animal escaped, at which time Pan and Lester then assisted and would not give up tracking until the wounded animal was down. Sometimes a hunter would get buck fever and freeze without getting off a shot, but he always got another chance. After taking a good ribbing from Pan, he would be mentally alert and ready the next time.

When the partnership broke up, Lester took over the area on the south slope of the Ilgachuz and Itcha mountains, and Pan retained the area on the north side, where he used the Home Ranch as a base camp. That way he could keep an eye on the ranch operation.

The guiding business was sort of hit and miss at first as Pan did little to promote it. He relied mainly on word of mouth advertising, which produced only two or three hunts a year, but it did help supplement their income. Rich Boland had met Pan and the family when he was just a youngster; his mother cooked for Rich and Gloria Hobson on their Rimrock Ranch. Rich, then eight remembers the visits well, when Pan, Betty, Willie, and Diana came to visit the Hobsons for a few days. Rich, with his family, moved around B.C. and Alberta, but thinking about the Blackwater. Finally, at age 14, in 1957, he wrote Pan, asking if he could come to work, but only for room and board.

Pan had taken a shine to the lad and agreed. Rich joined the family at the Anahim Stampede that year and a pattern was set; he became a part of the family and recalls, "Pan treated me like a son from that first summer on."

For the first two winters, Rich left to work in the logging camps, and was sorely missed. It was inevitable that the next year, he should ask to go along with the hunting parties to help. Ultimately, Pan got him an assistant guide's license and from then on, he remained at the ranch, or in the mountains with Pan, during the winter.

Diana worked in the hunting camps, too, and obtained her license, thus she could dub in as a cook, or go along as a guide. However, Pan was very protective of his attractive daughter. Diana laughs about it today, "I finally figured out that Dad was taking me along only when the hunters were older men, not when the young good looking fellows showed up."

Peter Alexis was a regular assistant guide. Frank Sill, Floyd Vaughan, Barry Rempel, Toby Cave, Dave Halgonberg and George Chantyman were others that helped guide through the years. If necessary, one of the other licensed natives would fill in.

Pan eventually had to accept the fact Richard was no longer a kid, but a man and as such, could make far more money logging than he could as a ranch hand, or guiding. So he made Rich a partnership deal, offering him half interest in the guide-outfitter business, if he would build two mountain hunting cabins and cut the wagon roads to them. They were now full-fledged partners and Pan began treating Rich like a man, instead of a teenage kid.

Cutting wagon roads into the mountains is hard tedious work. Days of riding, searching for the best possible route, preceeded the falling of hundreds of trees and clearing brush. It was back breaking work, as all the trees had to be cut low enough so wagon axles could clear the stumps, and bucked up small enough to move by hand. Pan knew this, and if Rich's finished road was passable for a chuck wagon, Pan had no complaints.

The job building a log cabin, suitable to sleep six or more people, provide room for stoves, tables, chairs, cupboards, etc., wasn't a small task either. Splitting the puncheon for the floors and ceiling was exasperating as the jackpines usually had a twist in the grain, refusing to be split straight down the middle. That meant every board had to be hand hewn with an adz. There was no doubt in Pan's mind but what Rich earned his half interest, which not known to either of them, would net Rich a sizeable sum, when he sold the business to Gus Able, a few years down the line. And that did not take in consideration his fifty'fifty split of the profits each year.

Another cabin was built by Barry Rempel, Diana's husband, and Dave Halgonberg, for Pan in the Itcha Mountains. It took them all summer to cut seven miles of road and put up the cabin.

Outside privies were 'two passenger convertibles,' and if it snowed during the night, Pan handed a broom to the first person going that way. One thing, there was never a waiting line to use the outhouses, because no one lingered in the snappy temperatures.

Richard and the assistant guides did the wrangling. Pan looked after the cabins, cooking, and the B.S.ing with the hunters. Richard would be out saddling the jingle horse, long before Pan arose. Whatever was left over from the night before was scrambled with eggs and served for breakfast. As Dieter Berg told us, "There were sure some God awful concoctions passed out."

Leo Lillienwise was bull cooking at the camp one fall, and Pan was in town for supplies. Leo sent Richard into the mountains with two Oregon hunters, an old Indian woman for cook, two cases of beans, and "not a hell of a lot more." Four days later, Pan arrived with the additional grub and the men told him, "Boy, Leo sure has impressed us for life." Pan just grinned, Richard wisely held his tongue, and the cabin door was left ajar for the next few nights.

Len Pickering remembers either Pan, or Richard, attending the Western Guide-Outfitters Association conferences, representing their outfit. Pan told Len they supported the organization because there was a definite need for lobbying on behalf of the guides. "It's a tough row to hoe. Seems like the environmentalists are all agin us," Pan said.

Pan had to learn how to treat his hunters as the times changed. His first parties we're hustled into the saddle the day they arrived, putting them into camp stiff and sore for their first morning's hunt. Pan was all business and didn't see the need to feed and pamper them the extra night at the ranch house, but in later years, he softened his attitude and when they operated out of the fishing camp, he usually let his customers lay over one day. This gave the men time to get acquainted with the horses, adjust the stirrups, and take short rides to limber up their muscles. Pan's customers became pampered and the hunts became tame, a far cry from the wild and woolly camp outs during his days with Lester.

At the fishing camp, Diana did the cooking, with some help from her Dad who really wasn't a bad camp cook. Once though he was almost at his wits end during a trip with Toby Cave along as an assistant guide. They had elected to tent instead of using any of the mountain cabins, and had chosen a nice little valley, with a stream, for the night's stop. Toby began setting up camp and Pan busied himself by setting out the grub and cooking utensils, discovering he had forgotten the frying pan. He thought on this problem while he joined the hunters in a drink, then while they had their second round, Pan built the fire high, sat back and watched it die down to hot coals. Then he flipped the steaks on the hot embers, turning them quickly to sear in the juices, then he had another drink, turning the meat once more. The Americans thought it was the best steak they had ever tasted. "Couldn't do it again, if I tried to," he whispered to Toby.

Pan instructed his assistant guides to let the hunters do their own shooting, but the first time Diana guided a man, her new license burning a hole in her pocket, she was tempted to ignore her Dad's words.

A group of Americans flew in, in a twin engined Aero Commander. Pan, as usual, was proud as punch when the fishing camp strip was used by a large aircraft. Gordon Bennett was one of the group and Pan assigned Diana to guide him. "Picked me out a happily married man, like always," Diana grumbled to Rich. Pan, Peter Alexis, Rich, and Diana comprised the crew for the four hunters. As they relaxed the first night in camp, Pan and Diana collaborated on the evening meal and all of them had a few drinks, but then turned in, anxious to get out hunting the next morning early. Diana was far more eager than the rest, for this was to be her chance to prove herself as a guide.

They were in the country Diana knew like the back of her hand. She wanted to help Gordon get his moose the first day and she wanted her Dad to be proud of her.

Two hours later, they were eyeing seven cows and calfs and a young bull, which looked like the answer to any hunter's prayer. But the animal didn't stack up to Gordon's expectations. Also, he wasn't keen on ending the thrill and fun of the hunt so soon. He didn't shoot, making Diana upset. "Hope to hell you like Spam," she clipped.

"Why?"

"Cause, by God, that's all yer gettin' tonight."

Gordon thought she was kidding, but that night Pan let her have her head, and she dug deep in the chuck wagon until she found the spam cans - and that's what they had for supper.

The story did have a happy ending. All four men got their trophy bulls, and as much meat as the Aero Commander could lift off the airstrip.

There were times when Pan would enlist the aid of a bystander to help pull off one of his pranks, "figgering " Yankee' hunters were all fair game. Such was the case in this episode. Once again the scene was the Log Cabin Court, in Quesnel. Pan had rented a unit and the party was in full swing. Doc Holley, Art and Dude Lavington, along with a couple of cowpokes no one knew, were among his guests. Pan could not resist inviting anyone that came by, to bend elbows with him.

In the next unit was a Seattle hunter, so Pan being neighbourly, stepped over to invite him in for a drink, too. The man had shot a moose and it was packed in his trailer outside. It must have been his first kill, for he continually bragged about his prowess as a mighty hunter, which eventually bored the others.

Pan winked at the Lavington brothers and suggested they go get some steaks for supper. Catching Pan's cue, they were on their way. Meantime Pan poured all another drink. "Tell us once more how you shot that critter. I might have missed somethin' the first few times you told it," he asked the 'great white hunter.' And the story was told again.

During which time, Art and Dude were busy in the parking lot. They trimmed the hide back on a succulent hind quarter of the Seattlite's moose, and cut several big, thick, steaks. Then they laid the hide back down on the quarter, tied down the tarp, found some newspapers to wrap the steaks, and returned in triumph to the party.

"Damn. Thought you guys would never get back. Think I'm getting a bit deaf in one ear - keep hearing the same noises," Pan said.

The units had kitchenettes and Pan soon had the steaks sizzling in a frying pan. They all gorged themselves, including the hunter, agreeing the meat was the best they could have had. And the man didn't wise up that it was his moose meat, which tasted so good, until the conservation officer rolled back the tarp, to do his inspection at the Cache Creek station, the next afternoon. Word traveled back, they weren't sure whether the hunter was going to laugh or cry.

Pan and Rich visited Ed Adams at Sleepy Hollow one season, taking along an Oregon hunter. There they discovered the man had pulled a 'No-no' by bringing a hand gun across the border. Understandably, not one person can now remember his name. However, when Pan found out, you can rest assured, the man was told what a fool he was to tempt the strict Canadian gun laws. Pan didn't harp on the subject so there were no hard feelings, and the cheerful bull shit spread in the glow from a coal oil lamp hanging from a beam over the table. Later the subject of illegal weapons came up again. The man pulled the hand gun from under his coat, took the clip out, checked it, then shoved it back in. Pan had no sooner got the words, "Put that damned thing back in its holster," out of his mouth when the 45 calibre automatic accidently fired, the bullet imbedding into the cabin roof. But the concussion had blown out the lamp and as the gun forcibly ejected the spent cartridge casing, it smacked Pan in the chest, at his open shirt front.

Ed had given up for the day and was lying on his bunk, the covers over his head. When the shot went off, dousing the light, he jumped up like he had been turpentined, yelling, "What's happening!"

Pan found his voice and started kiying, "I've been shot I've been shot!" Rich struck a match, lit the lamp again, expecting to see Pan slipping slowly to the floor, with blood oozing everywhere. The hunter froze in his chair, wide-eyed, what thoughts going through his mind, God Only Knows.

"Hell, yer not shot, Pan. The spent cartridge must'a hit you. There's where the bullet went, right into the roof," Rich told him.

Pan was a little sheepish about the incident and laughingly said, "I knew I wasn't shot - jist wanted to give our dumb friend here a scare." Who really got the scare? You be the judge.

"Pan never broke a deal after shaking hands."
—— Gordon Wilson

MOVING ON

Troubled by his illness, mentally and physically tired of the hard ranch life, and of a mind to try something different, Pan began contemplating the sale of the Home Ranch. Too, Betty had been down with arthritis and had to go to a Vancouver specialist for several operations. The last few winters, he had noted Diana and Betty seemed depressed with the isolation, they all were edgy and quarreled a lot.

"I jist don't want to put in another winter like that. Gonna sell that damned place, lock, stock and by-God," he told Toby Cave in the spring of 1969. He ran several advertisements, and got three serious replys. One was from Bob Anthony, a Utah sheep man, who wanted to do a bit of pioneering, plus become a cattle rancher. He and his wife Dorothea, flew into the Home Ranch, took a cursory look around, asked a few questions and said. "We'll take it."

Diana sat down to the typewriter and made up an agreement of sale that Pan, Betty, the Anthonys and she formulated. One thing - with no ranch hands in the bunk house at the moment, there was no one to witness their signatures, which bothered Diana, but not Pan, who was used to a man's word being his bond.

After the Home Ranch being his home for 35 years, Pan Phillips was to leave by May of 1970. He didn't voice any second thoughts at the time, but down the line, he thought perhaps he shouldn't have sold.

However, Pan was not at a loss as what he was going to do and he told Betty, "Now we can get on with the fishing camp plans."

Betty thought about that statement, mentally visualized the work it would take to start over, plus the cooking and cleaning for the fishermen each season, and decided with her physical condition being what it was, she would move into Quesnel. There she could set up a place where Pan could spend his winters.

Diana chose to stay with her Dad, helping Rich to get the finishing done on the camp and into operation, as well as work as a hunting guide when Pan needed her. Rob choose to go with his mother, he wanted no more of ranching, either, and would look for a job in town.

In the spring of 1970, Anthonys moved in and the Phillips family moved out.

Rich, anticipating his partnership in the fishing camp, as well as the guide-outfitting business, was already living in the first cabin he and Barry had built on the site near Tsetzi Lake. Ed Adams, who by then was considered a family member too, had moved to his own place at Sleepy Hollow, one that once belonged to Happy Thompson.

After Anthony bought the ranch, a large log lodge building, plus four additional cabins were built. He planned to turn it into a working guest ranch, which Pan had agreed might work, but somehow it didn't, regardless of Pan's support.

The cattle operation didn't turn out to be the financial success Bob had hoped for and it wasn't until he had re-sold the place, that Pan received all his money.

"Pan was fair in all his business, he just dealt to the
bottom dollar."

— —Floyd Vaughan

THE SECOND AIRSTRIP

The initial deposit money from the Home Ranch sale
in his pocket, Pan was ready and eager to start his plans for
the fishing camp on Tsetzi Lake. He knew he had to have a
good usuable airstrip dozed in after the cabins had all been
built. For the project he called on his friend, Toby Cave, an
excellent bush pilot, to check the land and 'walk-out' an
airstrip. Toby found the ideal place between Tsetzi and
Airplane Lakes, behind the cabins, a slight uphill grade to
the south.

Floyd Vaughan and John Blackwell, partners in Moose
Lake Lodge at that time, owned a D-8 cat, so Pan
approached them on building his airstrip. In September,
1971, the two men 'walked' the machine through the bush
from Moose Lake and broke ground. Meantime, Rich was
busy finishing cabins, with Diana, Barry and, sometimes,
Rob helping.

Floyd's wife, Laura, moved over with their children
and set up tent camp. Floyd began hauling in diesel for the
cat in his Stinson, landing in the pasture below the
proposed airstrip. He hauled in three 45 gallon drums at
one time, plus filling one of the plane's fuel tanks with
diesel, as well. However, the big loads and the hard
landings on the uneven ground, took their toll on the plane
and before the job was done Floyd had to retire it with a
damaged landing gear.

John finished the airstrip and collected the agreed
upon price from Pan. To say that Pan got a bargain would
be a gross understatement.

The following summer, Pan and Rich opened the camp
for business. Pan was excited and happy as the airstrip
came into use, but his biggest thrill was to come, when a
DC-3 landed and took off. For his own enjoyment, he kept
an accurate count of the plane numbers and their
nationality, in his lodge guest book.

Veera Bonner received a letter in 1982, in which Pan
stated, "The latter part of July, I had 38 planes in. Thirty
three were on wheels and five float planes. One week end
we had 109 people in, the cook and I was sure busy keeping

everybody fishing and happy."

Undoubtedly, the happiest of them all, was Pan.

The Pan Phillip's Fishing Camp airstrip hasn't survived without incidents. One arrival proved more than spectacular as a passenger in a Piper Tri-pacer, becoming acutely aware that the plane was about to land short, decided to get out and walk - while the plane was still in the air. Luckily, he fell into a swampy area and was able to walk out reasonably intact. The plane did land short and sat off the runway edge for a considerable time awaiting repairs.

Pan witnessed the whole performance, and as usual, only had this to say, "Jesus Christ! Built over a half mile of airstrip and he can't hit it."

Another aircraft sat out the winter waiting for a new wing to be delivered and installed. This accident happened this way. Early one morning, Jake Malic was landing his twin engined Cessna 310 when he spotted two horses running out onto the runway from the bush. He tried to steer the plane between them and the edge of the strip, but caught the left wing tip on one horse's rear. The aircraft yawed to the left, but he managed to salvage the landing, however was shocked to see one wing half gone, gas dripping from the tank.

Pan came running out, very excited, and as soon as he knew Jake and his passengers were okay, he went looking for the horse. Fifteen minutes later Pan had the horse in the corral, sans injuries, but soaked with gasoline and mighty shaky from the experience. Two pails of water, soap and a good scrubbing ended the trauma which could have been far more tragic.

Pan's hearing was excellent, and he could detect the sound of a plane long before the average person. The minute he heard the sound of an engine, he would run out to see who was coming by. If the plane landed, he was right there to greet the passengers when the prop stopped. Diana swears she had actually seen her Dad knock over chairs in his haste getting out to the strip before the plane landed.

His running days on the wane, Pan bought a three-wheeled Honda, which brought a standard joshing remark, "That's a funny looking horse you're riding."

"Beats the hell out of walking or runnin', and I don't have to cut hay for it neither."

"Pan tried to be everyone's friend."

—— Dieter Berg

TOGETHERNESS

One thing life in the Blackwater led to, during Pan Phillips time there, was togetherness.

Wherever he stopped for the night when on the trail, he was always welcome, but might have to share a one room cabin with a man, his wife, three kids, one dog and a couple cats. Jumping into a bunk with another person was the norm, if he was lucky enough to find a bunk.

Unless he was out on the cold trail, and common sense forbid it, Pan was inclined to sleep in the nude, and in line shacks, or hunting camps, many were the times he was accused of 'mooning' someone, when he got a nature call.

Bob Anthony decided to throw a party for Pan, Betty and his new found friends in late 1970. Betty flew out from town and Pan rode over to the Home Ranch from his fishing camp. The party was going full bore into the wee morning hours, a few people straggling off to their assigned sleeping quarters. In a total state of relaxation, Pan looked about the room for Betty, and saw she was gone. Feeling a bit amorous, he decided it was bed time and pussyfooted off to the bunkhouse by the creek where they were to sleep. Stealthily he entered, dropped his drawers, shucked his boxer shorts, then leaped into bed, grasping for Betty.

A loud shriek, a kick in the groin, a push, and Pan found himself sitting, nude, in the middle of the floor, as a flashlight came on to disclose Betty and Mickey Dorsey, Lester's wife, staring wide-eyed at him from the bed. "You keep your grubby hands off me, Pan Phillips! Put your clothes on and get in the other bunk!" shouted Mickey.

Betty had a few choice words for Pan too, then considered the source of the problem, shrugged, and went back to sleep.

"Jesus Christ! Jesus Christ. Sorry, Mickey," was all Pan could think of to say. He pulled his clothes half on, carried the rest and went back to the party for the rest of the night.

On Pan's now famous trail ride of 1975, from Tietown to Anahim Lake, the second night out, he decided we would need some moose meat to carry us over on the ride, so he dispatched Bill Solowoniuk and Rich Boland on a ten mile ride over to a ranch to see if they had any extra meat. The participants began to smell a rat, when they saw Rich combing his hair and heard him ask Bill for a clean pair of socks.

Pan watched and listened, a faint smile appearing on his face. From the chuck wagon, he brought forth a bottle of CC for the fellows to take along, as payment for the moose. Mistake #1985479. Bill and Rich mounted up and disappeared in the waning light.

Supper was over, and pitch black outside the campfire reflection. Several hours later we heard horses approaching, their riders singing, yahooing and laughing. The errant cowboys rode into camp 'hell-bent-for-leather' and behind them came a very attractive young lady,* riding a roan, her long black hair flying. Behind her came one tired dog. They still had a bit of CC left, but not much. However, they did have the moose meat - and the girl, and were grinning like cats that had just discovered a saucer of milk.

The trio's arrival revived the trail riders, and the bull session around the campfire lasted for hours, boosted by additional bottles of CC, Pan the center of storytelling. Shortly after midnight, the young gal allowed as to how she would have to hit the trail back home.

"Hell," Pan spoke up. "No use in doing that this time'a night. You kin bunk with me. Got plenty of room in my bedroll."

"Bull shit, Pan Phillips. I'd rather sleep with a grizzly bear," she retorted, indicating she wasn't sold on togetherness.

Pan "Hee hee"-ed to his tent, as she tightened her saddle cinch, jumped on her horse, and disappeared into the night.

---

* We have deleted the young lady's name. Somehow it seemed the thing to do.

Her departure was the topic of breakfast conversation - all knowing that the girl had a ten mile horseback ride, in pitch blackness, without a gun, or anyone to protect her.

Pan hadn't given it a second thought, a girl alone, at night on the trail. She was a product of the country. By the time she left, Rich and Bill were too limber to ride and no one else offered to escort her home.

Her dog, still tired, had elected to stay where it was warm and comfortable, and the girl apparently had forgotten him. Thus we were stuck with the pooch for the balance of the trip. Pan worried about the dog, especially when we rode into Anahim Lake and he had to fend off the village pack to protect it. Somehow, this didn't seem to bother Rich or Bill much, and they both volunteered to drop off the dog, at the girl's on their way back. Wonder why?

"Pan had to hear the noon radio messages come hell or
high water."

—–Rex Bartlett

THE FISHING CAMP

Pan settled in at the fishing camp and seemed to enjoy
it immensely from the first day on. It was less work than
the ranch and he liked meeting the new people that flew in.
His partner, Rich, swung the logs for the additional cabins
and Pan slung the bull with the customers. The fishermen
liked Pan's stories, especially when he talked about his
experiences with wolves; Pan hated the animal and
relished telling how he had eliminated a pack or two. He,
also, spun yarns about the caribou and moose he had seen,
photographed, and shot; of his experiences in packing the
meat on a spooky horse; and his early days in the
Blackwater, pioneering the Home Ranch.

But there was one story he only told if someone
insisted on it. Pan was convinced he had once met up with a
Sasquatch, cousin to the Indomitable Snowman, or the
Yeti. "People'll think I'm off my rocker," he'd say. So we
won't tell it either.

When the lodge building foundation was laid out, Pan
didn't have a tape measure handy, so he staked off what he
felt would be the right width and length, using a light rope.
Rich put down the first round of logs and discovered
something was amiss with Pan's stakes. The foundation
blocks were set out of square, by about three feet. Then
Rich remembered - the day Pan did the measuring, the
wind blew and neither one of them had noted that the wind
had bowed the rope out on one side. With considerable
colourful language, Rich tore the crooked side out and did
it over, as during any building process, Pan seemed to find
another chore that needed attention, a customer that
needed help, or a sudden call to the outhouse - anything to
keep him away from work.

Pan had a knack for enticing people to help him
without asking, or offfering to pay. Notable among the
donors were Bill Solowoniuk and Leo Lillienwise, who
spent much of their spare time at the lodge, doing any odd
task that needed attention. When we asked Bill why, he
replied, "Damnfino. I just liked Pan and he was sort of a
father image to me. I enjoyed helping him."

Leo's answer was similar, except he looked upon Pan more as a "bull shitting buddy."

The lodge and cabins were built on an old Indian campground, where the natives came to net their winter's fish supply in the small creek. Several 'kickwillie' indentations were still visible, where the natives dug a deep circle for the base of their temporary dwelling. Pan swore that at night he heard the ancient ones, pounding teepee stakes, especially on clear, quiet nights. But Diana, Rich, and the others scoffed, until they were all aroused from a deep sleep by the same noise, which Pan had been describing. Toby Cave was in camp, he ran out on the porch to listen. "That's no damned marsh bird, or whatever you think it is! That noise is coming from the Indian camp site."

No explanation was found come morning, or since. Toby admitted the eerie sound sent a chill up his back. "Thought I was bull shitting you - didn't ya?" Pan snorted.

Since Pan supplied the cash for outfitting the camp with boats, motors, tackle, bedding, etc., he did his usual bargain hunting and they ended up having a wide array of different makes and models of both the boats and outboard motors. The only thing similar about the boats were that they were all flat bottomed. "Don't want anyone water skiing and using up all our gas - these won't go fast enough," Pan told Rich.

Keeping the motors running was another problem. As Pan put it, it was "plumb exasperating," mainly because he was about as mechanically minded as a Missouri mule and about that stubborn, too. His theory - if a nut, screw, or bolt didn't turn easy, force it, something would eventually give. When Rich was away hunting, Pan's patience sank to a low ebb. That was when any volunteer, who happened by, was given a wrench. Sometimes it was a successful manipulation of free labour, but if the volunteer knew as little, or less than Pan, the motors didn't always 'purr' afterwards.

One time, Pan bought a new Japanese make. Upon unloading it from the plane, he immediately took it to the rickety dock, over the creek. There he tightened it on the framework erected for testing motors, gave the rope a pull, and the outboard purred like a kitten. Rob and Leo stood on the bank watching. Pan cocked one ear, listened, then told the two, "Got some kinda funny noise in it. Sounds like they forgot to tighten up a nut inside. Go get the tool kit, Rob."

Pan laid the motor in the grass and on getting the tools, began to dismantle the engine. Within seconds, a spring 'twanged' into the deep grass. Soon it was followed by a screw that Pan dropped. "Hell, probably don't need those anyway," he opined. Fifteen minutes and the motor was completely apart - parts scattered. "Seems, I've misjudged those Japanese. This motor looks okay. I'll put it back together after lunch." Pan turned towards the lodge.

Leo and Rob immediately began a search, on their hands and knees, for the missing parts, hoping to get the motor reassembled before Pan had a further chance to tinker with it. But Pan wasn't that long at lunch and returned before they finished. "Here, I'll take over. I kin remember how it went together better'n you fellows."

The men stepped back, shook their heads, rolled their eyes, and hoped for the best.

The cover back on, the motor looked as good as new, but when he again tried to run it, it shook so badly that the cover flew off into the middle of the creek, the vibration broke the board holding it, and the whole caboodle fell into the water, sinking to the muddy bottom. "Jesus Christ. Jesus Christ," Pan moaned. "Rob, shuck yer clothes real quick and find that motor. It cost too damned much to lose."

Rob, in working for his Dad, had learned not to say "Why?" when Pan told him to jump to it, just "how high?" so he shed his clothes on the run, jumped into the creek and began diving for the motor. After much floundering, he brought the cover, then the engine to the surface.

Rob made a quick run to the warm cabin. "Kid looks like a drowned muskrat," Pan grumbled, referring to Rob's long, wet hair and beard. "Don't know what this damned world is coming to - men growing hair long like a woman." His remark reflecting his distaste for the fad among the young men.

Turning back to his problem, he turned to Leo, smiled and said, "Looks like you got a bit of work cut out for you. I'll be in the lodge if you need me," and strolled off.

Leo tells it now with a smile, but he wasn't smiling then.

We would be remiss not to mention one small item that bugged the cabin builders at the camp, with the exception of Pan. That being the sites. The fishing camp area took in about an acre between the airstrip and the winding picturesque creek, which meanders between Airplane Lake and Tsetzi Lake, creating ideal niches for the cabins thus keeping them somewhat private. But Pan wanted them all in a straight line - so straight in fact that you could look from one cabin to another, to another, to another, through the windows, as only about 20 feet seperated each building. Pan didn't purchase such frivolous things as curtains, so when it was a co-ed camp, dressing and undressing posed a problem of privacy. "Spent good money to buy glass so a person could see the scenery, so why the hell cover them up?" was his stock answer.

Wayne Reavis, a good customer and friend of Pan's from Medford, Oregon, once asked him how he got the large, plate glass window into camp for the lodge, noting it was too big to be flown in by the average plane. "Sent a wagon in for it. Told them jist how to fix the glass between bales of hay, with hay underneath the edges. Worked fine except the damned fools didn't bring in any hay that we could use for feed, they used old, rotten bales. No damned horse sense atall."

The sign that greeted us when we landed at the Pan Phillips resort, was indicative of the man - creative and amusing. It read:

Pan Phillips International Airport
World Flights Arranged
Dogpatch Delivery
Weekly Service
Honeymoon Trips Arranged

Diana spent considerable time, before and after her marriage to Barry Remple, doing the cooking and washing, during the summer seasons. Getting her Dad to shuck his jeans so she could get them washed was a chore and they had a continuous argument about the subject. "Those damned things are just too dirty for you to wear when you've got guests in camp. Take 'em off so I can throw them in the washer," she nagged.

"Hell no. They're good for a couple more weeks, yet."

This banter went on until Diana devised a plan. She had an un-house-broken kitten that loved to sleep on Pan's pants. Usually, he spied the cat before his pants were used as a litter box, but Diana set on this way to get the jeans washed. There was an odor in the pants, the little tom couldn't resist, so every time she sneaked the cat in, it would piss on Pan's pants. She counted on it. Pan would have to don a clean pair in the morning. Although he threatened the cat's life (all nine of them), he was a softie at heart and never carried it out. The kitten stayed unhousebroken, and Pan greeted his guests in clean jeans.

Each year, the camp customers were about 75% repeat visitors and to them, it was almost like coming home. Pan met them, then turned them loose, to take care of their boats, motors and own entertainment, while he sat back. Rex Bartlett, who owned a hardware store in the States, always showed up with items that would repair or replace something, having noted it on his previous visit.

Gordon Bennett's wife, Edith, loved to cook, so as soon as she was on the ground, she took over the lodge kitchen, cleaning and cooking most of the meals while they were in camp.

On a perfect fall day, we landed at the camp, traveling through the country from Fort St. James, to our home on Shuswap Lake. It was to be a half hour stop for coffee and visit with Pan. His daughter, Gayle, had left the week before to get her children in school, after spending the season as camp cook and housekeeper, so Pan was behind with the chores. Since the weather had been particularly nice, there were fisherman booked in for the coming weekend and none of the cabins were cleaned or the beds changed. Our half hour stop turned into a three day stay. Darlene became the camp cook and housekeeper and Jack the bull cook. Pan, as usual, held the coveted position of "spinner of tall tales."

Pan surely must have had a magnetic personality, for there was always someone around, working their fanny off, instead of sitting and being pampered. Many of Pan's close friends had a hard time paying for their stay. Regardless of his reputation for being a scrooge, he didn't want to accept payment from those who had spent their holiday working. Most ended up hiding their money where Pan would find it later.

Pan was thrifty in feeding his guests. Old habits being hard to break, the milk cans had only one hole in them, the coffeee cups were filled to the brim, and little leftovers were never thrown out. Diana chided him for this, to which he replied, "Money don't grow on trees, ya know. Do like I told ya." Hard and hungry times caused Pan to develop a fettish for not wasting food and every leftover could be put to some use, especially in a stew pot. One time when he had made a big stew, not all of it had been consumed, so he sat it aside on the kitchen cupboard and forgot it for a few days. Upon discovering it again he noticed a slight green tinge to the food and reluctantly, decided it would have to go for dog food. The dog turned up its nose at a helping.

"I'll be damned. It can't be that bad," Pan smelled, then tasted it. A few minutes later, Barry came in with two hungry bear hunters. Pan stoked up the kitchen range, added a healthy portion of tobasco sauce to the stew, heated it, and served it. Knowing Pan, Barry shied away from the meal, sticking to a sandwich. The hunters ate every bite, declaring it to be the best 'son-of-a-gun' stew they had ever eaten. Barry fully expected them to beat the grass down to the outhouse, however, it didn't seem to affect them at all. Everyone was happy, most of all Pan, who had managed to salvage "some good grub."

Pan, also, had his own system to conserve coffee. The pot was always on the stove, any visitor was welcome to a cup, but he still worked to save every drop. Left over coffee didn't get thrown out, nor did all the old grounds. He just removed some and added fresh grounds to the remainder. It turned out to be a tasty brew, suprisingly few complained.

Pan was over 60 when he put in his first garden at the fishing camp, having shunned that task at the Home Ranch. When the results of his efforts popped from the ground, he took a keen interest and his yearly garden became his pride and joy. Fish guts, as fertilizer, produced fantastic results, and everytime he gazed at the abundant crop his eyeballs registered dollar signs from thoughts of the 'grub money' it would save.

The food bill was a thing Pan paid close attention to and he didn't always see eye to eye with the cook placing the orders. If there was a cheaper item he could substitute, he crossed off the higher priced one, adding the other. This led to words, often not pleasant ones. Gayle once ordered a few cans of beets, knowing that her Dad didn't like them, but the customers would. The order got mixed up and a full case was sent out, which gave Pan a fit. "What the hell you gonna do with a whole case of that hog food?" He fussed and fumed for days.

On the next order, Gayle used the same list, doing a few additions and deletions. When the plane delivered the groceries, she discovered another full case of beets, she failed to delete them from the list. Beets became a standard fare on the camp's table for many meals, Pan making sure they were used up so there was no "damned waste of money."

The resort had many famous people stop by and Pan took it all in stride, very seldom getting flustered. However, when a fellow flew in with a Playboy centerfold model and an airline stewardess, he was pretty excited, retiring to his own cabin to don a clean pair of jeans and comb his hair, followed by a quick trip to the creek to rinse off his china clippers.

This may have been Pan's first introduction to 'Pot' but those girls and their companions, were not strangers to it. They carried the packages with them and convinced Pan he should take a couple of puffs, which he did to keep face. We heard of only one other time when he was forced into a similar situation, where he felt it prudent to go along with the majority. He was definitely against the use of hard core drugs, but remarked, "Since marijuana don't seem to hurt people, I really don't see the harm in smoking it and I'm not about to blow the whistle on anyone."

Once, with Thanksgiving fast approaching, Pan was alone at the resort expecting a lonely holiday, when he heard a plane arriving. As the aircraft parked, he was there to greet the arrivals, scarcely believing his eyes as they climbed out. There were the Chilcotin Airways pilot and four ladies, Betty Rhodes; Hazel Henry, whose idea it was to be there; Hilda Mortimer, formerly with CBC; and

Veera Bonner, a freelance reporter for the Williams Lake Tribune. All were old friends, and had he rubbed Alladin's magic lamp, he couldn't have done better. Happily, Pan gave a big "Whoopee," kissed and hugged each in turn.

The ladies arrived early Saturday morning and stayed until Monday afternoon, bringing enough food for their Thanksgiving feast. None of them had known Pan to be religious, but at the dinner, he asked that one of them say grace, whether to appease himself or them, we don't have a clue.

He was the gallant host, taking his guests to visit the Home Ranch, showing them nearby water falls, visiting his neighbours, the Lamberts, and providing the means for their fishing expedition. Hazel and Hilda wanted to leave their catch for him, but when they unloaded in Williams Lake, he had hidden them aboard.

As a result of Veera's visit, there appeared a full page of pictures in the comunity section of the paper, on Pan and his fishing camp. He was proud as punch.

As it turned out, Pan wouldn't have been alone that weekend, for several other parties flew in, thinking he needed some company. It took him a week to get the smile off his face.

Pan didn't condone fishing in the spawning stream that ran through the camp's grounds. "The stream's for those over 65 and under six," he said. But he made an exception for Edith Bennett. Pan enjoyed her cooking and was impressed by the apron she wore in the kitchen, so much so, he gave her full run of the place. For years, he watched the jean clad women and Edith's apron added a touch of femininity he appreciated.

Pan managed to keep his 'cool' under situations that called for strategy, but Bill Solowoniuk recalls one time when Pan had a difficult time controlling his temper. Bill and Pan went to the fishing camp to open it for the season. When they arrived, they found a plane parked, cabins and shed door locks broken, and several men using the fishing equipment. Pan, shaken and pale, fought to control his rage. When the men returned from the lake, Pan took them aside. Bill couldn't hear the conversation, but when Pan came back to the lodge, he was still so upset, he had trouble breathing. Still he managed to handle it in a

PAN THE GRACIOUS HOST, sat at the head of the table at the resort, never letting the CC bottle get too far from his reach, especially if one of the guests happened to be furnishing the joy juice.

diplomatic manner. The cost of the locks, hasps, and damage was on the fishermen's bill when they came in to settle up.

In 1978, Pan bought a CB radio, antenna, new batteries, gas powered generator, and a charger. This opened up a whole new field of activity for him as he spent hours 'rubbering' (listening in). But the main event every day was the noon messages broadcast by the Quesnel Cariboo radio. Pan demanded quiet from anyone and everyone so he could hear every word. It was his substitute daily newspaper, plus his contact with customers and family, in lieu of daily mail.

Things didn't always run as fine as sifted flour at the fishing camp. Leo, Rich, and Pan and Gayle were relaxing in the lodge awaiting the next aircraft to arrive carrying customers. In the conversation, Gayle brought to Pan's attention the fact that the propane refrigerator wasn't working too good, but he allowed as how if it was still keeping things cool, what could go wrong? "No movin' parts in the damned thing anyway."

The topic was changed by Leo, who was in the middle of a giggle, after telling one of his slightly off-colour jokes, that had brought a flush to Gayle's face, when there was a loud explosion and the entire room filled with soot. "Scared the crap right out of us," he recalled. Everyone pushed for the door at the same time, causing a pile up. To this day, Gayle swears her Dad ran right over her on the way outside.

Pan preferred life at the camp, as opposed to the hunting outcamps, so he traded his half interest in the hunting business for Rich's half interest in the fishing camp. In turn Richard then rented a cabin for his hunting base and cooked for his own customers. Rich, wanting to go into logging, sold the hunting area to Gus Abel who in turn, sold it to George Betemps, who still operates it (1985). So the fishing camp operated with two 'cook shacks' until George moved his base camp to the now empty Home Ranch buildings. Pan continued cooking for his customers until the lodge propane refigerator exploded, then he advertised, "Bring yer own grub." The arrangement seemed to work out fine.

A major chore was in keeping the lodge floor clean. If the cook, or her helper, or Betty on a visit, scrubbed the kitchen and the main room, Pan ignored his muddy boots, but if he had done the cleaning, it was a whole new ball game and he had a few hundred words to say to any individual who left dirty tracks.

The customers laughed about Pan and his 'forever quitting smoking' tactic. After announcing his intent to quit, it wasn't long until he reverted to his panhandling days of yore and was forever bumming a cigarette from customers and crew. "Gimme one last smoke," he would say, but a few hours later when withdrawal symptoms began to hit again, he approached someone else. The crew figured it was too much when he complained about the brands they smoked, and he mooched, but the visitors laughed and those that were repeats, brought extra smokes with them, knowing Pan would put the bum on them.

Pan looked out the lodge window one day, to see Linda Harrington, daughter of his long time friends, Ronnie and Betty Harrington, come riding into camp. She was on her way home from the Anahim Lake Stampede and was hot, dusty, and tired. Pan was on the porch by the time she was tieing her horse to the hitching rail. As usual, his greeting was cheerful, Linda knew the welcome mat was out for her at Pan's anytime. "You look sorta tuckered," Pan said. "Why don't you go take a good hot shower and relax? I jist filled the barrel with hot water, but I kin take a shower later - go ahead and use it."

It was an invitation Linda couldn't refuse, she dashed off to the shower stall. Pan yelled after her, "There's not too much water in the tank so you'd better get under it before you turn it on."

Inside, she quickly kicked off her boots, shucked her clothes and stepped under the shower head. Having used it before, she was used to the home made gadget that allowed the water to cascade down from the barrel on the roof. Linda pulled the handle and gasped, then screamed. The water was ice cold, as he had just filled the tank from the creek, and the sun hadn't warmed it yet. Pan's bath really wasn't due for another day or so. The people in camp, who had run up, after hearing her scream, could faintly hear Linda cursing inside, but could really hear Pan's loud "Hee hee"-ing outside.

There was a whole group of fishermen and guests sitting around the barbecue pit. The fire was just right to bake the succulent trout laid on the grill. Pan squatted near it. Carol Berg happened to glance across the fire and saw a gas can nearby, leaking. She yelled at Pan, "For Christ sakes, Pan, move that gas can before we all get blown up!"

"Hell, woman, it won't explode, just leaking a little like that. Watch this." Pan struck a match, on his thigh, and tossed it at the can. Carol and the others, who had caught the remarks, leaped backwards in one big tangle. "Hee hee. It's only water," Pan snickered. For a spell, Carol gave serious thought whether to shoot him, push him in the creek, or both.

The victory party, celebrating Alex Fraser's election, as Mayor of Quesnel, was swinging, when someone brought it up that "Pan Phillips isn't here to help us celebrate." "Hell, let's just move the party on out to his place at the lake," Dieter Berg told the group. Thus it was that Pan watched in amazement as a single engine Otter and a Cessna 185 unloaded a total of 17 people, unannounced. The party hardly missed a beat, resuming at the fishing camp, with Pan now in the middle of the festivities.

For two summers, in a row, Pan had a group of college people staying at the camp. They were an adult class from Toronto's Huber College, instructed by Richard Rumble. The nine students tented away from the cabins; cooked their own meals; spent their time studying the flora and fauna; boning up on general ranching in the west; or listening to Pan spin yarns about the country. In general they were quite self sufficient. When it came time for wood gathering, or haying, they pitched in to help with the work, even though Pan received payment from the college for their stay and the information imparted to them.

Again, Gayle was the cook. "You hardly knew they were around, unless you needed some help and then they were Johnny on the spot to assist. A nice group of people. Dad enjoyed them and heard from some for a long time after their visits."

Pan had a favourite trick to pull on first time guests. He would come running out of the lodge, towards whoever was standing about, yell, "Hey Joe, (or whatever his name) yer wanted on the phone." Then when the man ran into the lodge, Pan "Hee hee"-ed and slapped his leg in delight. Upon realizing he had been fooled, the guest came sheepishly out of the lodge. Pan would disappear for awhile.

Bunch Trudeau came by to visit quite often and this one time she had a group of friends with her. They were drinking coffee around the lodge table, a steady conversation humming. Pan flitted from the kitchen to the table, asking questions about the outside world whenever he could get a word in edgewise.

GENTLEMAN RANCHER/RESORT OWNER. Once Pan had all the kinks out of the fishing camp operation he took things rather easy. No more daylight til dark spent on a mower or hay rake. At the resort he still had a chance to keep his hand in with horse drawn equipment, and the work would always keep til the mood struck or the weather co-operated fully. Pan figured there was "Always tomorrow".

At Pan's request, Wes Carter had brought in a box of firecrackers, which might not have proved to be a favour, it could have earned Pan a punch in the nose, that day.

On a trip to the kitchen for the coffee pot, Pan hesitated behind the partition, lit a string of the firecrackers, and unnoticed, tossed them under the table. The scramble, as they exploded, sent him into hysterics, "Hee hee"-ing and slapping his thigh as he raced for the back door, before Bunch could gather her wits and get to him.

Once in a while Pan got a good laugh out of life without any planning on his part. Here is the story he often told about John Blackwell and Wayne Escott, a Dean River Air Service pilot.

John and Wayne landed in a float plane and tied up at
the Tsetzi Lake dock. Seems Pan had sold John a propane
refrigerator and the only way John could get it over to his
Moose lodge was to hire the Beaver aircraft on floats. The
two men proceeded to carry the heavy fridge from the
cabin porch to the lake, stopping often to rest. At the lake,
they moved slowly onto the dock, Pan kibitzing from shore.
As they got alongside the airplane, a loud creak and crack
eminated from the boards under their feet. Suddenly the
dock collapsed.

Pan told it like this. "Both of 'em dropped into the lake,
into loon shit up to their knees. The fridge, after falling in,
came to the surface, and began floating away, then sank
again. They had a helluva time getting it back out to shore.
John and Wayne both had a few thousand words to say to
me about my rickety dock, but I don't know what was eatin'
them - I had the dock to rebuild, and besides, they could do
with a bath anyhow." He had a twinkle in his eye each time
he re-told the story. Probably, what irritated Wayne and
John the most was Pan, standing, dry, on shore, laughing.
John didn't ever get the fridge to work right after the
dunking.

Wes Carter, from Amboy, Washington, flew into Pan's
for fishing on a few occassions, and began to work up a yen
for the country. Pan's enthusiasm for the Blackwater was
rubbing off on him and eventually, Pan was instrumental in
his buying Ed Adam's spread, in Sleepy Hollow, three
miles over the hill. Ed was to remain on the property as
long as he wanted to. Came the day to firm up the deal. Wes
picked up Pan and Ed in his Cessna 180, flying them into
Prince George where a lady attorney was to handle the
paper work. Her waiting room was small. Wes sat reading,
Pan sat fidgeting and Ed, getting a touch of claustrophobia,
paced the floor. Plus Ed worried because he had forgotten
to bring the deed.

Finally, they were ushered into her inner office, where
her first question for Ed, as the seller was, "What's your
name?"

Ed is hard of hearing and as a result speaks quite
loudly at times, so he bellowed back, "By God, I didn't
bring 'er with me. Plumb fergot."

"Jesus Christ," Pan chimed in. "Now she's gonna think
were trying to take advantage of some old coot that's sick

in the head."

The attorney turned her back on them for a moment, to admire the scenery out the window, her shoulders shaking with silent laughter she fought to control.

Wes used Pan's airstrip and came in at odd times, whenever he could get away from business. On one occasion, no one from his place was there to meet him, so he asked Pan if he could borrow a horse.

"Sure, I'll go fetch ya one," was the instant reply.

Pan showed up a few minutes later, leading Scotty, an old rodeo horse, now in his 'string.' He pointed to the tack on the rail and stood by watching Wes saddle up. "Better lead him out a bit from the cabins before you fork him," Pan advised, after noting Wes had overlooked a twist in the cinch.

Wes, thought the remark odd, but did as Pan asked. When he put his foot in the stirrup, though, he knew why, as the rodeo began. Scotty threw him, high, wide, and hard onto the ground. Pan grinned, like a hound trapped in the meat house.

"Ya gotta pay attention to little things like that," pointing at the twisted leather. Wes muttered an unprintable reply, dusted himself off, and checked to see if everything still worked.

In 1981, Wes decided to give up his idea of becoming a B.C. rancher and returned to the States to live. Pan bought the ranch from him, where Ed Adams continues to live today (1985).

It worried Pan to see the RCMP plane circling for a landing, but he was at the strip when the engine stopped. He soon found out why they were there, a young constable handed him a summons.

"Who the hell's this Floyd Phillips?" Pan asked, he hadn't seen that name in print since he had become a Canadian citizen. In reading the summons, and being supplied information by the "Queen's Cowboys," Pan learned the story.

Pan lent his name and prestige to Bob Anthony's Home Ranch promotion, wherein Bob proposed to sell the new cabins and the land on a time share basis. However, an RCMP investigation had alerted Consumer Affairs personel, who discovered the cabins actually sat on crown land and not on the deeded land Pan had sold to Anthony.

Pan was summoned to Victoria as a witness, for the crown.

Dieter Berg, also, a witness, and Pan traveled to Victoria, via a party or two in Vancouver. At Victoria, Pan put up at the Frasers and Dieter stayed in a motel, but in the evenings, they all got together and moved the city over an inch or two. One bash led to a 'Volkswagen Cram' eight people in all, Pan stuffed in the back, on the bottom.

At the trial, Pan was relaxed, grinning and joking. The people in the courtroom seemed to know who he was and he reveled in the attention shown him.

When the dust of the trial settled, Anthony was off the hot seat and Pan had protected his investment. Dieter hadn't gained much, except having a good time and enjoying Pan's company.

Rita Anderson was one of the last camp cooks for Pan, in 1982. She had a super sense of humour and Pan used to kid and banter with her. One afternoon, Diana and Rose Cassam had ridden in from Sleepy Hollow. They all sat drinking coffee, when Pan began teasing Rita, she returning barbs as good as he gave. Finally Pan said, "Hell, you needen't worry. I'm too old to cut the mustard anymore."

"Yeh, but you're not too old to play in the mustard jar!" Rita retorted. A red faced Pan fled the cabin.

"Pan had to ride every day. When he was laid up, it was pure hell."

—Jack 'Happy' Thompson

LIFE'S UPS AND DOWNS

At the isolated Home Ranch, minor illnesses and injuries were treated with home made remedies, when the first aid kit failed to supply a known treatment. The concoctions ran the gauntlet from a mixture of kerosene and honey to cow dung poultices.

Pan was never one to complain and put up with aches and pains, either from working in the cold; hard jolts in riding; a whiplash from tree limbs; cracked knuckles; or numerous other ailments that would have laid up a less sturdy person. He did anything he could to avoid going to a hospital, or doctor, and even the word 'operation' scared him. He went to naturopathics and chiropractors, trying to avoid doctors, except socially, when he could, as he grew older.

Each serious injury was a climactic experience, both for the injured person and the family members and ranch hands. Life was held by a thin thread, sometimes, the distance and weather playing a major role in the dramas. It was a miracle that only one life was lost, that when Len Cave was killed in the plane crash.

In 1963, Pan's whole body swelled up. There certainly wasn't anything in the first aid book, or kit, to diagnose the problem, so arrangements were made to fly him out to the Quesnel hospital. Careful examinations disclosed Pan suffered from a glandular problem and with the proper medication, he wouldn't be laid up too long.

Toby Cave was in town, boarding with Art Lavington and both came to see Pan at the hospital every night. Rich and Gloria Hobson drove down, from Vanderhoof, to see him, and the Frasers were regular visitors. Even with the attention from his friends, Pan began badgering the doctors to let him go home, when they did, Toby flew him out.

On January 24, 1968, Pan was headed for Anahim Lake on his snow cruiser. There was two feet of fresh snow and the big machine bogged down, or tipped over, time after time. Conditions for snowmobiling were at their poorest, and the skis kept pushing up the new powdery snow, like a snow plow. Under his heavy clothing, Pan was soaked with sweat. Every bone in his body ached from wrestling the heavy machine. Then he started to have chest pains. When he finally reached the road, he was about done in. The first pickup that came by, stopped and the driver, noting Pan's condition, tried to persuade him to park the snowmobile and ride on in to Anahim Lake with him.

"Thanks a lot. But I've ridden this son-of-a-bitch this far so I'll ride'er on in."

But he only made it to the Holte's at Lessard Lake. Realizing, Pan was terribly ill and possible in the throes of a heart attack, they insisted he stay the night, making him as comfortable as possible. Andy's daughter-in-law, Teresa, sat up with him all through the night. Pan continued to have pains in his chest and left arm, which made her feel helpless, as there seemed little she could do for him.

Basically Pan was in fair health, but the stress of tugging on the heavy snowmobile precipitated the attack. It was the beginning of his heart problems.

The next morning, the Holte family make preparations for taking Pan into town, but he bowed his neck and was determined to continue on the snow machine, at least to Clesspocket. Unable to sway him, Andy started it for Pan, helped him on the seat, and watched him off down the road. At Clesspocket, friends (we are not sure who they were) took matters into their own hands and loaded him into a highway gravel truck. They then drove in a snowstorm to the top of the Tweedsmuir Park grade where they met Ken (Willie) running the Department of Highways grader. Pan was helped into the grader cab, and Ken took him down the steep switchback road to his pickup, parked on the valley floor. They raced into the Bella Coola hospital.

Pan had had a heart attack. They kept him there until March. But Pan was itching to get out, within days of his confinement. The doctors were adament, so he tried to make the most of his predicament.

Happy Thompson and a few other friends, who were in The Bella Coola area, stopped by to visit and he tried to bribe each one into bringing him a drink, but they balked, for Pan's own sake.

Losing that round, Pan began to work on the doctors and hospital staff. "Let one of my friends bring me a bottle and I'll keep it outa sight." he pleaded. Finally, to satisfy him, one of the doctors called Doc Holley, in Quesnel, and asked what he thought. Holley, knowing Pan's thriftyness, replied, "Hell, yes, let him have all he can drink....providing he buys the hooch himself!" and chuckling, hung up. The Bella Coola doctor sensed there was a good joke in the remark someplace, but not knowing Pan's aversion to spending an unnecessary dime couldn't put his finger on it.

The first week in March, Diana drove the team and sleigh into Anahim Lake to pick up her dad. Ken brought Pan over the mountains, from the coast, in his pickup, to meet her. Pan insisted that Diana ride the snowmobile home and he would drive the team. The sleigh, being Pan's freighter, was fixed with a box like contraption up front, hay spread on the bottom and an open slot in the front for the reins to run through, that way, he could lay in the warm hay out of the wind. With a lighted lantern to heat the shelter, Pan was fairly comfortable.

During the nights on the trail, Diana kept a watchful eye on her Dad for fear he might have another attack. The second night, she repeatedly got out of her bedroll to lean over him, listening for his breathing. Once she couldn't make it out, above the noise of the wind, and excitedly began to shake him. When he roared, "Whatinthehell's the matter with you?" it was music to her ears. Three days later, they drove into the yard, arriving March 9th. Three tense days for a young girl.

Pan stayed on the Home Ranch until the fall cattle drive. He thought, then, it might be a good idea to have Doc Holley check him over, so he called him from Alex Fraser's house. The doctor was just about to leave on his annual hunting trip, however, he told Pan he would stay over a day, instructing him to "Get your ass in here early in the morning and we'll see if you need a tune-up."

Pan's physical turned out good, Doc Holley telling him he was in pretty good shape, for the shape he was in, then he wrote up a list of instructions for Pan, seriously contemplating each entry. Pan stood nervously by, like a kid waiting for a report card, expecting anything from large doses of castor oil to a turpentine enema. When he read the list, though, he broke out into a wide grin, it said, "No young stuff. No fancy stuff. Don't get too excited and only go to bed with your own wife. Drink all the booze you can get Alex Fraser to buy for you." This time the thrifty stigma was thrown onto Alex.

Following his accident with the horse and traps, Pan's medical problems began. From that time, he had poor circulation in his legs and developed varicose veins, some that raised a half inch on his legs. In 1969, he flew into the hospital to have them stripped. Pan laid around for a few weeks in town after the operation, then decided he could make it okay and went back home.

In an early May day, 1978, Pan was organizing things for the season at his fishing camp. He began to feel sick, but tried to tough it out, feeling worse each day. Francis Cassam, one of Pan's good native friends,didn't help matters either. He rode over for a visit, tied his horse to the hitching rail, walked in, peered at Pan and said, "Oh, I seen somebody look like you before. He die." Which did not ease Pan's mind.

By 10 p.m. that night, he used the CB radio to call Diana and Barry at Sleepy Hollow. Luck was on his side, they were still monitoring the radio. Cassam had stopped by earlier on his way home, told them how Pan felt, so they had deliberately left the set on.

Pan said he needed them, and an airplane to take him out in the morning. Through Moose Lake Lodge's radio phone, help was arranged for, and Diana saddled up her horse, rode over the mountain, and spent the night with her dad.

George Dunlap, from Quesnel, flew in early. There wasn't any medic available to accompany him, so Sandy Unger, the camp cook that summer, jumped into the plane to help. Pan's lips seemed to be turning blue, causing them all to fear another imminent heart attack.

Because the weather had turned sour, George had to divert to Williams Lake, and Pan was put in intensive care. Again he made a quick recovery and soon was back at the lodge catering to his fishing buddies from all over the Northwest.

Late summer, 1981, Pan again began to feel punky,

and the occasional chest pain was worrying him. He got progressively worse, until again he had to call for help on the CB. Ole Moody, taking care of Wes Carter's place, intercepted Pan's message and again called Moose Lake Lodge, they in turn got through by radio phone to Floyd Vaughan, who flew out in a helicopter immediately, bringing Sister Suzzane from the Anahim Lake Nursing Station with him.

Barry, in Anahim Lake for supplies, heard the message and was at the nursing station when the helicopter arrived. They kept Pan there for a couple hours, then decided he needed more care than they could give him. Floyd transported Pan into Williams Lake in the Beaver. He was placed in intensive care.

Diana, and her three boys, rode over to Pan's , there John Blackwell picked them up in his float plane, taking them on into Anahim Lake, where she borrowed D'arcy Christensen's pickup and drove the 200 miles to Williams Lake. Only the family was allowed in to see him, but he was resting comfortably. Mickey Dorsey's visits cheered him the most, because she claimed to be his sister, thus was able to see him every day. And Pan did appreciate her pulling a fast one on the hospital staff.

Out of the hospital, Pan went to stay with Betty in their mobile home in Quesnel. Upon feeling better, later in the winter, he elected to go to Victoria and visit the Frasers, Alex by then being an MLA and Minister of Highways.

Alex and Gertrude were planning to go south, where Alex was scheduled to undergo chelation treatments at the Doctor Saccoman Clinic in El Cajon, California. "What-inell is chelation treatments?" Pan inquired. Gertrude explained that they removed placque residues (cholesterol) from the arteries; in essence it was a blood cleansing treatment. When he showed interest, Alex asked if he would like to go along.

"Hell, yes. I'd like to go. Sure can't do me any harm." Ten days later they were at the airport ready to depart. Pan had given them many reasons why he would prefer to travel by bus or train, but Alex figured it was mostly because the dollar signs were flashing in his eyeballs. Gertrude asked Pan if he had any extra medical insurance for the States travel, he said, "No." So she herded him into an insurance office where he, reluctantly parted with ten bucks, that later would prove to be the best investment of his life.

The clinic's treatments were on a daily basis for a month, and took up a greater share of the days. but the trio did get some sightseeing in and enjoyed a holiday of sorts.

By the time the treatments were over, Pan had had enough of big city life and all the people, he was ready to go back home. Their return was booked on a direct flight to Vancouver, however, the jet's engine malfunctioned during the run-up on the taxiway and the hassle of getting them on another flight began.

Pan became extremely agitated, he was afraid his connections, by bus from Vancouver to Quesnel, would be thrown all out of whack. Once on the plane, he did relax somewhat, seemingly happy to be on his way.

But they had to change planes in San Francisco. As usual in the terminal, time was of the essence as their connecting flight departed from another gate, at least a half mile away. In the part trot, part walk, but hurry, hurry situation, Pan's face became red and flushed and they had to stop a couple of times for him to catch his breath. Gertrude flatly stated there were other flights, and the haste wasn't that necessary, again Pan said "No" and continued on.

Alex and she were just a step ahead of Pan, when Gertrude heard him make a noise. Looking back, she saw Pan collapse and heard his head hit the floor. His call had been for help.

Being an RN, Gertrude, without a doubt, saved Pan's life. She immediately dropped to his side, removed his false teeth, then began CPR. Alex tried to keep the curious crowd back and asked if there was anyone who could help her. Two young men stepped forward, assisting her, with obvious knowledge of CPR, too.

Ten minutes later, a doctor arrived, followed in a few minutes, by an ambulance crew with a stretcher. The medics and doctor then worked on Pan for about twenty minutes more, before they took him to the waiting ambulance.

He was still alive, but "His colour was the shade of a grimy white bedsheet, and his attempt at breathing came only in spasmodic gasps." Gertrude is positive that Pan had "died" and the CPR brought him around again.

Pan hovered between life and death for two days, the Frasers always at his bedside in the hospital. Slowly, his condition stabilized, and relieved that their long time friend was on the mend, Alex and Gertrude departed for Victoria. Ken (Willie) and Betty had caught a jet as soon as they got word, Betty in a wheelchair after her own operation. Pan's youngest sister, Hazel and brother, Joe, flew in from Illinois to be at his side. By that time, Pan was out of intensive care and in a three bed ward, but still fuzzy and confused by the sedatives. It took him some time to recognize everyone, however, he seemeed to improve rapidly once he knew they were still all there.

When his insurance was about ready to run out ($18,000.00 worth) he was badgering the doctors to "Open the corral gate and let me outta here."

On November 26th, Ken and Betty got him back to the Quesnel mobile home. He spent the rest of the winter there, recuperating under the care of Doctor Calder. As spring arrived, he was chewing at the bit to get back to the fishing camp.

"Talking with Pan, or being around him, always gave
you a lift in life."

——D'arcy Christensen

WHAT ARE FRIENDS FOR

During the Home Ranch days, Pan's 'outside' trips, to
visit people,were few and far between. The family did get
back to visit his relatives in Illinois and his sons in
Wyoming, but it wasn't until he had the fishing resort
established, that he found time to wander in the off season.

Upon closing the camp each year, he would settle in
with Betty, but since he just was not used to city life, it
wouldn't be long before he got itchy feet and would think of
someone to go visit. He had many friends in Quesnel,
however, his closest friend, Alex Fraser was 'politicin' in
Victoria, so Pan did not see him as much as he would have
liked.

Alf Legler was one person Pan spent many hours with,
Alf lives (1985) in a retirement home near the hospital.
They swapped stories of the 'old times' and reminisced
about friends, while having an occasional game of
checkers.

Bill Solowoniuk's place became a second winter home
for Pan. Betty drove him there and Bill took him home. Pan
liked the quietness on Bouchie Lake, the countryside felt
more like the Blackwater. Bill's young children took a
shine to Pan, and he to them. When Bill had to drive to
William's Lake on business, Pan would go along. Although
there was considerable difference in their ages their
philosphy was the same and they got along good.

Another old friend, Art Lavington, lives (1985) seven
miles out on the Barkerville road and Pan managed to
hitch a ride out to see him, several times, "For a cup of
Lavington coffee, strong enough to float an anvil." These
visits were times of reminiscing and, of course, an
inspection of Art's horse, which has become more of a
house pet than a saddle horse.

Leo Lillienwise lives (1985) within a rifle shot of Pan
and Betty's mobile home. Pan spent a lot of time with Leo,
"Jist gonna run over and share a few giggles with him," Pan
stated to Betty. One winter, Leo talked Pan into taking an

extensive snowmobile trip, 'bumming around the Blackwater,' and when asked where they stayed nights, Pan replied to the city dweller, "Damned poor man if you can't find a bed in that country."

Toby Cave lives (1985) in Quesnel, he usually was the one who flew Pan out during the winter to check on the cabins, lodge, and horses every few weeks. Pan spent many hours discussing his fly-in trade with Toby.

Ken and his wife, Andrea, and the children live in Williams Lake (1985). Pan took the bus down, spending a few days at a time. The older he got, the more he seemed to take a shine to his grandkids, and he loved to be around them.

One visit Pan tried not to miss was the 'Overproof Classic,' held at Doc Holley's place. Invitations went out to a rather select group, Pan among them. Each year, sometime between Christmas and New Years, Holley harnessed up his dog team, and Tom Moffatt, Pan's friend and Doc's neighbour, hitched his horse to a cutter. The race was on, winner take all - all the booze that he could drink, that is. (Side bets expected and accepted.) On that festive occasion, Pan didn't bother going home at night, afraid he might miss something.

Pan was a picture buff and each year he tried to borrow additional slides and photographs, taken around the Blackwater and Chilcotin area, so he could show them at the Done Roving Seniors Home to the people he often referred to as the 'old folks.' Some were younger than he was. He, also made slide presentations at the Senior Secondary School to an enraptured group of young would-be cowboys and cowgirls.

His mid-winter fidgets caused him to travel not only in B.C., but the States. Most any excuse would do. Pan made several trips to Vancouver on one pretext or another. Once, he checked into a hotel, on Hornby Street and set up a meeting with Gus Abel, who by then owned the guide business, Pan and Rich worked, the rental of a camp cabin for Abel's base cook shack as the reason.

Another time, Pan heard that his old cohort, Rich Hobson's wife Gloria, was in Vancouver, recuperating from an illness. Again a perfect excuse to get out of Quesnel and the mobile home.

George Atkins lives (1985) in Sooke, Pan paid him and his wife, several visits. Upon his arrival, George hurried to the grocery store buying ice cream and fresh strawberries by the gallon, recalling they were Pan's favourite desserts.

Pan, also, dropped in on Elaine, her husband, Al Biggan, and their children, as well while on the Island. At first, they lived in Prince George, but moved to Glen Lake, near Victoria (1985). On these visits, Pan liked to travel with Al, who is a cash register repairman. While Al worked, Pan would bend the ear of the store owner, making friends in the process.

A frequent winter visit, was at Alex and Gertrude Fraser's place, where he spent many comfortable and reminiscing hours with them.

From what we were told, not only was Pan welcome, but those he visited were delighted to have him. Seems that when Pan arrived on the scene, wherever and whenever, the place lit up. Around Pan, life was vibrant.

In 1977, Veera Bonner, and her sister, Hazel Henry, laid plans for a bus trip around the southwest of the U.S. Through correspondence, Pan found out about it, and decided to join them as far as Phoenix, Arizona, where he would visit his brother Fred (now deceased), and then go on to Illinois to see the rest of his family. Pan had a ball escorting the two gals at the bus stops, seat hopping to make new acquaintances, and spinning his Blackwater yarns. While in Arizona, Wes Carter, and his wife, Jorja, flew down in his 180, to join Pan. They made the round of all the tourist traps, Pan particularly enjoying 'Old Tucson' a make believe western town used as a movie set. There he was in his element, as he trod the rough plank floors and sidewalks, leaned on the hitching rails, and jawed with the tourists and workers, dressed in western garb.

Pan took all his slides and photographs with him on that trip, and the fact that his family and friends took a keen intrest in his B.C. 'pioneering' days, pleased him. He needed no urging to 'show and tell.'

Once while at Rex Bartlett's, in Marysville, Washington, they decided to take Rex's 36 foot cruiser, Holiday, across to Victoria - the purpose was to see Frasers. Being it was February, the weather was not exactly condusive to yachting and they had to lay over three days in the San Juan Islands, due to rough water. Rex told us that Pan took it all in stride, including the rough water, saying, "As long as it isn't rough enough to spill my drink, t'ain't bad."

Wes Carter's home in Amboy, Washington, was Pan's destination on a couple trips south, one with D'arcy Christensen and on one of his own in 1982. Pan felt comfortable and at home there, and as Wes said, "Pan could watch me work all day. Never seemed to tire him a bit."

He liked the constant re-runs of old western movies, he never found them boring. If Wes was away on business, Pan found a favourite chair and spent hours in front of the 'boob tube.'

On the jaunt with D'arcy, they not only went to Carter's, but to see Bob Anthony, in California, and Wayne Reavis, in Medford, Oregon. Whenever they stopped, D'arcy said "the women flocked around Pan, showering him with hugs and kisses, genuinely glad to see him."

Nearing home, at the U.S. and Canadian border, D'arcy pulled into a tax free liquor store, to pick up their allotted 40 ounces each. Somehow, while D'arcy looked over the merchandise, Pan wandered out, got on the wrong side of the building and fence, becoming confused. When D'arcy found him, Pan was so excited it scared him and he ran for the car's trunk to get Pan's medicine out of his luggage, fearing Pan was about to have another attack. For the rest of the trip, he kept a sharp eye on Pan, shielding him from further excitement.

Pan was with D'arcy, another time, on a fur buying trip, by aircraft, in the northern hinterland, around Vanderhoof. They borrowed Dieter Berg's pickup in Vanderhoof, and lit out the Kenny Dam road, contacting trappers in the bush. It was pouring down rain, so they got stuck on a Stoney Indian Reserve dirt road and had to leave the truck. Walking to the nearest house, D'arcy again fretting that Pan could become ill over their problem and exertion. But at the house, the people had heard of Pan and the welcome mat was out. In that friendly atmosphere, Pan relaxed.

In the early spring of 1983, Pan was telling everyone about his next planned visit, coming up in the winter of 1983-'84. "Goin' to visit the Browns, over in Anglemont," he said. "Gonna write up my 'autibiography.' We're gonna bull shit in the mornings and then while Jack and Darlene write in the afternoons, I'm gonna go down to the Senior Centre, shoot some pool and B.S. with the 'old folks'."

Pan didn't make it.

"Pan could enjoy himself, no matter where he was."
——Dave Dorsey

THE LAST WINTER

The die was cast for Pan's last winter when Dieter and Carol Berg flew into the fishing camp, to spend a night with him. Alex Fraser had talked to the Bergs by phone, telling them that Pan had not been well. Good friends that they were, Dieter and Carol decided to take a holiday and go see Pan.

When they arrived, Pan was alone. Betty, who was out for a few days, had gone over the mountain to Sleepy Hollow to see Diana, Barry and the grand kids. So over the usual 40 oz. bottle of O.P. rum, the B.S. session began. Pan was complaining that he hated to see winter coming on as he wasn't able to stay by himself at the lodge all winter. He was at loose ends on what to do.

"I don't like it in town and I don't like the trailer, it's too damn confining, to suit me." He went on to tell them he had applied for a caretaker's job at one of the local lodges which had a radio phone.

At that point, the Bergs chimed in, "We need someone to take care of our lodge and pub while we're away on holidays." "And Carol needs help fending off pub customers while I'm off on a winter construction job." Deiter added.

Pan's eyes lit up like 'a pair of fried eggs in a slop bucket.' He was sure interested, so the winter was set. The Berg's left and in the ensuing months several messages were sent Pan, setting a date in October for him to set out for Takla Lake Rainbow Lodge and Pub, 125 miles northwest of Fort St. James. Carol picked him up in Quesnel, checking with his doctor on his general health, his diet, medication and etc., leaving nothing to chance.

Dieter's plans were changed, so after Pan settled in, there wasn't much for him to do, except carry in firewood, so he established a favourite spot in a chair by the radio phone, where he "learned more about the Indians, their way of life and how they handled their money than he had in all the 47 years neighbouring with them in the Blackwater."

A phone call later in the month, advised Pan that his sons, Rob and Ken, were having a problem with the grazing leases at the Sleepy Hollow ranch. That caused him to spend some sleepless nights, regardless of Dieter's and Carol's assurances it was a minor matter, easily settled by phone. But unable to relax, he caught the weekly train south and straightened out the matter. Along the way, he picked up on the fact that D'arcy needed help in branding cattle and the old cowboy spirit soared past all Pan's common sense, weak heart or not. However, D'arcy wasn't about to let him overdo, so the trip to Anahim Lake not only was good for his moral, but probably didn't hurt him physically, either.

Pan arrived, via the train, back in Takla Lake, prepared to fullfill his commitment, to find not only had Dieter's construction work fallen through, but so had their holidays. Feeling that now he would be just extra weight around the lodge, Pan wanted to leave, but the Berg's were adamant in their decision he should spend the winter with them. So he stayed on, relaxing in his favourite chair by the radio phone and spinning tales for the odd visitor that dropped in.

A quick trip to Quesnel, in early Dec. was to see Betty and the kids, then he returned to Takla Lake for the Christmas holidays. He stayed until March, during which time he stopped smoking and seemed to be making headway in regaining his health. Carol had him on a diet, too, and he had lost the paunch he carried for so many years. Pan was concerned about his health and his future, he kept it no secret that he feared death.

His letters, to us and others, mailed from the Lodge, seemed to indicate he was enjoying his stay very much and there was not a hint but what he was carrying his share of the work load. Pan couldn't bring himself to admit he was just sitting around being pampered.

"I feel richer for having known Pan Phillips. He made me feel I was touching a part of the pioneer spirit, through him."

——Gordon Bennett

END OF THE TRAIL

ONE OF THE LAST PICTURES OF PAN, still astride a horse, only you'll note that he's traded his rifle for a pitchfork. Obviously he hadn't saddled up just for the fun of it.

There were several forest fires burning in the Blackwater area in May, 1983. The Forest Service had two fire supression crews and a helicopter stationed at Pan's fishing camp, renting cabins because of the central location, the float plane dock on Tsetzi Lake, the helicopter pad, and the airstrip.

On Saturday morning, the 28th, Gordon Hames, Forestry Service 'Protection Assistant' Officer, who had known Pan for 20 some years, flew in to the resort with two other men, in a twin-engined Islander. Pan, as ever, was there to meet the arrivals, being 'Johnny-on-the-spot' riding his three-wheeler. There were two other gentlemen there, real estate people from Prince George. We did not find out the nature of their visit, but can only assume, since Pan had decided to sell the camp, that perhaps they were there to appraise and list it for sale.

Anyhow, lunch time found them all in the lodge, with Pan about to listen to the noon messages on the radio. He had one leg cocked up over his desk and yelled at the men to, "Hold'er down will ya? So's I can hear this thing." The group turned back to their talking, although in lowered voices, and could hear the messages being given out by the announcer, in the background.

Gordon heard a thump causing him, and the others, to swing about quickly. Pan was lying on the floor by his desk.

"Aw, come on, Pan. Quit your kidding around. That ain't funny," remarked one man, thinking Pan was up to one of his pranks.

"I don't think he's kidding," Gordon blurted out, bending over the inert figure.

Pan was not.

The men went to work, Gordon giving him CPR and one of his assistants giving him intermittent breathing. In a few minutes, Pan revived enough to try to talk, but then they lost him.

Larry Davidson, the Rota-Tech helicopter pilot, from Quesnel, took off immediately, for Sleepy Hollow to pick up Barry. He radioed from the air for additional help. When they returned to the lodge, it was apparent there was nothing more anyone could do - Pan was dead.

Over 350 people gathered in Quesnel's LeBourdais Park, on June 1, 1983, to say their last 'Goodbye' to their friend and neighbour, Pan Phillips.

But there was no normal obituary for Pan. Cariboo and Chilcotin newspaper headlines proclaimed in bold face type, some above a half-page or more, of pictures and story; "Hundreds Bid Farewell To Cariboo Legend," "Gone But Not Forgotten," "Pan Paid His Dues," and "Top Hand Rides Over The Great Divide."

Truly a great tribute to a man we were lucky enough to have included among our friends.

In July, Pan's last wish was carried out. He requested his ashes be scattered over Kluskus, the long abandoned Indian village he camped at so many times. No one knows for sure why he selected that site instead of the Home Ranch, or his fishing camp, unless it was because of the beauty of the place. The old church and graveyard, the serene setting in the beautiful valley at the end of the Kluskus Lake chain, could capture the heart of anyone. Perhaps, Pan thought he would like to rest forever in the tranquility.

Toby flew Betty and Rob's wife, Teresa, out to the camp. Rob, Ken, Andrea and their two sons, Michael and Warren, were already at the lodge. Diana, Barry and sons, Jon, Wesley and Jamie, rode over from Sleepy Hollow. Floyd Vaughan came in with his DeHaviland Beaver float plane, from Nimpo Lake, to give Pan his final ride. It was a sad, sombre group, who boarded the aircraft for the flight over Kluskus.

There were no words spoken, just a silent prayer, in the heart of each one. Floyd throttled back, Rob rolled down the window, then let his father's ashes slowly drift from the urn. As they fluttered to earth, Floyd dipped the plane's wing in a final salute.

Knowing Pan, as we did, we can envision his big smile, from the beyond, as Floyd refused payment from the family for the flight. Pan's last ride was "On the house," and surely nothing would have pleased him more.